KT-502-195

# Sonnets, Bonnets and Bennetts

*by the same author*

THE FABER BOOK OF SMOKING

# Sonnets, Bonnets and Bennetts

## A literary quiz book

JAMES WALTON

writer and host of BBC Radio 4's
*The Write Stuff*

*faber and faber*

First published in 2008
by Faber and Faber Limited
3 Queen Square London WC1N 3AU

Typeset by Faber and Faber Limited
Printed in the UK by CPI Mackays, Chatham ME5 8TD



A CIP record for this book
is available from the British Library

ISBN 978–0–571–23937–5

2 4 6 8 10 9 7 5 3 1

In memory of Ted Walton (1929–2007)
A true quizzer

# Introduction

It's often said that we now live in a quizzing age – something to do with all the information we're bombarded with and can't use in any other way. Yet for some of us, this isn't a startlingly new development. In my own childhood, quizzes figured so prominently that, while other boys dreamed of becoming train drivers, firemen or footballers, I hoped that one day I might get to say 'Fingers on the buzzers, please,' to people who weren't actually members of my family (and who actually had buzzers).

The chance came in 1998 when I was asked to write and present Radio 4's literary quiz show, *The Write Stuff*. Many of the questions that follow are based on or inspired by the eleven series we've recorded since then – but none requires you to have heard, or heard of, the programme. All you need to join in is some literary knowledge, or even just literary interest.

As you'll see, every quiz here has five rounds. The first is what would count on the radio as a quickfire one (as in 'Fingers on the buzzers, please'). Next come six extracts to identify, which of course contain solid clues to the book and writer – but which, in most cases, are intended to be an entertaining read as well. After that, there's a round on a featured author: again aimed at the general book-lover, but with the occasional trickier question slipped in to test that author's true fans.

Round Four is at first sight (and possibly all subsequent ones) the most fiendish – where you have to find the connection between four literary people or things that might initially seem to have about as much in common as Oliver and Thomas Hardy, Sid and Henry James, Paul and Bamber Gascoigne, etc. (Please feel free to add any similar gags of your own.) As ever, though, the key to success is not to panic. If you take each of the four in turn, you should find one or two that provide the way in, and from there the rest will ideally fall into place. Each quiz then ends with another quickfire burst, this time with the linking theme (except for Quiz Ten) in the answers rather than the questions.

Meanwhile, as you'll see too, there's more to read than in the average quiz book. For the answers, particularly to the non-quickfire rounds, I've thrown in plenty of extra information that's meant, even for non-quizzers, to be satisfying in its own right.

Finally, just to protect myself against the purists: in the extracts, I've sometimes replaced a crucial name with a pronoun – or, to help with identification, vice versa. I haven't bothered either with ellipses for missing words . . . on the grounds . . . that this would make . . . for . . . too fiddly . . . a read. (See what I mean?)

James Walton

P.S. And just to protect myself a bit more, the title of the book is not, despite what some sharp-eyed readers might think, misspelt. 'Bennetts' refers to Arnold and Alan, both of whom show up at some point. It doesn't refer to the family in *Pride and Prejudice*, who only have one 't' – and who, anyway, are surely already covered by the word 'bonnets'.

# Quiz One

# Round One

## Literary Firsts and One-offs

1. Which literary character's first words to whom are: 'How are you? You have been in Afghanistan, I perceive?'
2. Which writer's first names were John Ronald Reuel?
3. Who was the first British writer to win the Nobel Prize for Literature – in 1907 if that helps?
4. Who was the first ever winner of the Whitbread First Novel Award, with *A Good Man in Africa*?
5. What was the first Harry Potter novel?
6. What's the only book for children by James Bond's creator, Ian Fleming?
7. Who's the only winner of the Nobel Prize for Literature whose first-class cricketing career is recorded in *Wisden*?
8. What are the first three words of Herman Melville's *Moby-Dick*?
9. Who wrote the 1984 novel *First among Equals*?
10. Who's the only person in literary history both to have been shortlisted for the Booker Prize and to have played a girlfriend of Ken Barlow's in *Coronation Street*?


Answers on pp. 19–20

# Round Two

## Pedants' Revolt: a Round of Literary Mistakes

In each of the following passages, the author has made some technical or factual error. Can you identify the author, the work – and the mistake in question? (If you should happen to be quizzing seriously, there's a point for the book, a point for the author and two for the mistake.)

1 'His specs – use them as burning glasses!'

Piggy was surrounded before he could back away.

'Here – Let me go!' His voice rose to a shriek of terror as Jack snatched the glasses off his face. 'Mind out! Give 'em back! I can hardly see!'

Ralph moved the lenses back and forth till a glossy white image of the declining sun lay on a piece of rotten wood. Almost at once a thin trickle of smoke rose up. A tiny flame appeared.

2 L–, light of my life, fire of my loins. My sin, my soul. L–: the tip of the tongue taking a trip of three steps down the palate to tap, at three, at the teeth.

3 Cannon to right of them,
Cannon to left of them,
Cannon in front of them
  Volley'd and thunder'd;
Storm'd at with shot and shell,
Boldly they rode and well,
Into the jaws of Death,



Answers on p. 21

Into the mouth of Hell
Rode the six hundred.

4 Antigonus: Thou art perfect then our ship hath touched upon
The deserts of Bohemia?
Mariner: Ay, my lord, and fear
We have landed in ill time; the skies look grimly,
And threaten present blusters.

5 This one appeared in the first edition only:

Stephen Wraysford's metal trunk had been sent ahead and was waiting at the foot of the bed. He unpacked his clothes and hung his spare suit in the giant carved wardrobe. The room was simple but had been decorated with some care. There was a vase of blue peonies on the table and prints of street scenes in Honfleur on either side of the door.

6 This is from a well-regarded novel of 2007, which begins one night in 1962 – but here flashes back to the summer of 1961, where a rock-and-roll fan is trying to educate his classical-music-loving girlfriend:

He brought to Oxford from the cottage a selection of records he wanted her to learn to love. She sat dead still and listened patiently, with closed eyes and too much concentration, to Chuck Berry. He thought she might dislike 'Roll over Beethoven', but she found it hilarious. He played her 'clumsy but honourable' cover versions of Chuck Berry songs by the Beatles and Rolling Stones. She tried to find something appreciative to say about each one, but she used

Answers on p. 22 

words like 'bouncy' or 'merry' or 'heartfelt', and he knew she was simply being kind.

(Clue: That night in 1962 is a wedding night)



Answers on p. 22

# Round Three

## Featured author: Jane Austen

1 In which county was Jane Austen born?

2 What did Austen's father do for a living?

3 In *Mansfield Park*, who owns Mansfield Park?

4 In *Pride and Prejudice*, what's Mr Darcy's first name?

5 Of which novel did Austen write in advance: 'I am going to take a heroine whom no one but myself will much like'?

6 What was the name of Jane's confidante and sister?

7 Which novel began as a sketch written by Austen in her early twenties called *Elinor and Marianne*?

8 To which public figure is *Emma* dedicated?

9 What's the fourth word of *Pride and Prejudice*?

10 What connects Jane Austen's tomb with a 1966 chart hit by the New Vaudeville Band?

 Answers on p. 23

# Round Four

## A Round on the Links: Literary Connections

Can you link the following literary people or things?

1 Peter, Susan, Edmund and Lucy are evacuated to the house of an old professor

William Blake's 'fearful symmetry'

Don Fabrizio, Prince of Salina, in a 1958 novel set in Sicily around a hundred years earlier

What's driven by the literary character whose first name (eventually) turns out to be Endeavour

2 *Interview with the Vampire*

*A Parliamentary Affair* (with a small spelling change)

Graham Greene's Viennese black-marketeer Harry **and** Tobias Smollett's Peregrine

Henry Williamson's bestselling otter **and** *Charlie and the Chocolate Factory* (with a small spelling change)

3 (If you get the fourth one here before getting the connection, award yourself at least twenty bonus points. Otherwise, try and work it out from the other three.)

The subtitle of John Keats's poem, 'Isabella'

 Answers on pp. 25–6

The main title of Benjamin Disraeli's novel subtitled *The Two Nations*

Peachum's daughter, who marries Macheath in *The Beggar's Opera*

The youngest son of John the Handsome in Volume Five of *The History of the Decline and Fall of the Roman Empire* by Edward Gibbon

4 Johann Wyss

A John Fowles novel of 1969

The sonnet sequence that contains the poem beginning: 'How do I love thee? Let me count the ways'

Michael Ondaatje wins the 1992 Booker Prize

Answers on pp. 26–8 

# Round Five

## Literary Festival: a Christmas Round

All the answers here contain, or indeed comprise, a word associated with Christmas.

1. Which country is the setting for Louis de Bernières's novel *Birds without Wings* – the long-awaited successor to *Captain Corelli's Mandolin*?
2. Who's the main character in Truman Capote's *Breakfast at Tiffany's*?
3. Which 1941 novel by Patrick Hamilton is subtitled *A Story of Darkest Earl's Court*?
4. What was Mrs Gaskell's first novel, subtitled *A Tale of Manchester Life*?
5. Which Austrian writer and thinker founded the movement known as anthroposophy?
6. Whose novels include *The Stone Diaries* and *Larry's Party*?
7. What was the first novel by E. M. Forster?
8. What's the only novel by Oliver Goldsmith?
9. What's the title of John Betjeman's blank-verse autobiography?
10. What's the most famous poem by Francis Scott Key?


Answers on p. 29

# Quiz One: Answers

# Round One

## Literary Firsts and One-offs

1 Sherlock Holmes to Dr Watson in *A Study in Scarlet* (1887). Holmes, as it turns out, is right about Afghanistan.

2 J. R. R. Tolkien

3 Rudyard Kipling – the second, should you be wondering, was John Galsworthy, author of the *Forsyte Saga*, in 1932.

4 William Boyd, in 1981

5 *Harry Potter and the Philosopher's Stone* (by, as you probably know, J. K. Rowling) in 1997

6 *Chitty Chitty Bang Bang*

7 Samuel Beckett, who played two first-class games for Dublin University in 1925 and 1926 – both against Northamptonshire. Beckett was a gritty left-handed opening batsman and a useful left-arm medium-pace bowler.

8 'Call me Ishmael.'

9 Jeffrey Archer

10 Beryl Bainbridge, who also holds the record for the person most often shortlisted for the Booker without ever having won. (Five times.) In 1962, she played one of Ken's fellow students, and a fellow believer in Banning the Bomb. Bainbridge, mind

you, is not the only person in literary history both to have *judged* the Booker Prize and to have played a girlfriend of Ken Barlow's in *Coronation Street* – because so has Joanna Lumley.

# Round Two

## Pedants' Revolt: a Round of Literary Mistakes

1 From *The Lord of the Flies* by William Golding. The mistake, now something of a classic, is (as all well-read opticians will know) that Piggy is short-sighted – and so the lenses of his specs would have diverged rather than concentrated the sun's rays. As a result, they could not have been used to start a fire.

2 The celebrated opening lines of *Lolita* by Vladimir Nabokov, where Humbert Humbert is explaining the phonetics of his beloved's name: Lo. Lee. Ta. Oddly, though, despite being no mean pedants themselves, Nabokov and Humbert have got it wrong. As the *Times Literary Supplement* quickly pointed out at the time, neither in English nor in Russian does a 't' sound tap at the teeth. It is, phonetically speaking, alveolar, which means the tongue strikes the gums where the roots of the upper teeth lie. Not only that, but surely the tongue doesn't take a trip of three steps down the palate either – from Lo to Lee it actually moves upwards. Do try this at home.

3 From 'The Charge of the Light Brigade' by Alfred, Lord Tennyson. In fact, as Tennyson discovered after he'd sent off the poem for publication, the number of riders going half a league onwards that fateful day was nearer seven hundred than six. Even so, he was unrepentant. 'Six', he said, 'is much better than seven hundred metrically, so keep it.'

4 From *The Winter's Tale* where Shakespeare gives land-locked Bohemia a coastline. Ever since Ben Jonson ridiculed this howler in 1619, critics have tried hard to explain it away: saying it's a deliberate sign to the audience that the play is taking place in a magical world, that Bohemia was a misprint for Bithynia, and so on. A more obvious theory – that Shakespeare didn't care much one way or the other – has maybe never been taken seriously enough.

5 From the first edition of *Birdsong* by Sebastian Faulks – and the mistake is a botanical one. Peonies can only be crimson or white, not blue. In later editions, 'blue peonies' was replaced with the cunningly vague 'wild flowers'.

6 From Ian McEwan's *On Chesil Beach*, based around a disastrous wedding night in 1962. Yet, in those happier days of their courtship, Edward couldn't have played Florence records by the Beatles or the Rolling Stones. By that stage of the summer of 1961, the Beatles hadn't released any, didn't get a British recording deal until 1962 – and, wouldn't record a Chuck Berry cover until 'Roll over Beethoven' in late 1963. The Stones, meanwhile, didn't play their first gig until July 1962. No wonder that in the paperback edition of the novel, the Beatles and Stones have mysteriously disappeared and Edward just plays Chuck Berry. Nonetheless, this seems a curious mistake for McEwan to have made, given that *On Chesil Beach* is set so carefully in the time that Philip Larkin described as being before 'sexual intercourse began/ In nineteen sixty-three/ Between the end of the *Chatterley* ban/ And the Beatles' first LP.'

# Round Three

## Featured author: Jane Austen

1. Hampshire
2. He was a clergyman (in Steventon, Hampshire. Jane was born in the rectory.)
3. Sir Thomas Bertram
4. Fitzwilliam
5. *Emma*
6. Cassandra
7. *Sense and Sensibility*, in which the two main characters are still called Elinor and Marianne.
8. The Prince Regent. In Austen's defence, it was a dedication she was more or less bullied into and very reluctantly made.
9. 'Truth' – as in 'It is a truth universally acknowledged, that a single man in possession of a good fortune must be in want of a wife.'
10. Winchester Cathedral – the name of their song and the location of her tomb.

# Round Four

## A Round on the Links: Literary Connections



1 BIG CATS

It's in the professor's house that Peter, Susan and the rest soon discover the Lion, the Witch and the Wardrobe – not necessarily in that order – in C. S. Lewis's novel.

'Fearful symmetry' is a phrase from Blake's poem 'The Tyger' – the one that begins 'Tyger! Tyger! burning bright/ In the forests of the night'.

Don Fabrizio is better known as the Leopard in the much-loved (and posthumously published) novel of that name by Giuseppe Tomasi di Lampedusa, about a Sicilian nobleman during the unification of Italy.

Inspector Morse, first name Endeavour, drives a Jaguar – although in Colin Dexter's early Morse stories, his car is a Ford Lancia. Perhaps more surprisingly, in those books Morse is also younger than Lewis, who at that stage was an elderly Welshman. It was only later that the success of the TV series made its influence felt on the novels – and the two main characters helpfully came to resemble John Thaw and Kevin Whately.

## 2 INDIAN FOOD

*Interview with the Vampire* is by Anne Rice, and so goes nicely with *A Parliamentary Affair*, the first novel by Edwina Currie. (Currie's novel came out long before the revelation of her relationship with John Major when he was party whip – but, by coincidence, it did concern an affair between a gorgeous female MP and a silver-haired party whip.)

Harry Lime was the black-marketeer in Graham Greene's *The Third Man*, and *The Adventures of Peregrine Pickle* was by Tobias Smollett. Put them together and you get Lime Pickle.

Similarly, Henry Williamson wrote the much-loved *Tarka the Otter* and *Charlie and the Chocolate Factory* was by Roald Dahl. Hence, with that small spelling change, Tarka Dhal. Unfortunately, Williamson didn't just stick to nature books. He also wrote passionately in favour of the Nazis – and in the foreword to his 1936 book *The Flax of Dream* addressed Hitler as 'the great man across the Rhine whose life symbol is the happy child'.

## 3 THE STAFF OF FAWLTY TOWERS

'Isabella: or the Pot of Basil' was a fashionably macabre narrative poem by John Keats, and a work he himself didn't like very much.

Disraeli's *Sybil: or the Two Nations* addressed the turbulent politics of the 1840s. (The two nations were the rich and the poor.)

Polly Peachum annoyed her father by marrying the local highwayman in John Gay's *The Beggar's Opera*. The play helped to make Gay successful enough to be buried in Westminster Abbey, where his self-penned epitaph is: 'Life is a jest, and all things show it;/ I thought so once, and now I know it.'

Finally, and almost needless to say, Manuel was John the Handsome's son – and himself a great soldier king – in Volume Five of Edward Gibbon.

## 4 EUROPEAN-COUNTRY-RELATED ADJECTIVES

Johann Wyss, a pastor by trade, became one of literature's great one-hit wonders in 1812 when he wrote *The Swiss Family Robinson*. His tale of a family shipwrecked on an island was primarily designed to teach children the importance of Christian values. It was also much influenced by *Robinson Crusoe* – which is presumably why the family has that not-very-Swiss surname.

Fowles's 1969 novel was *The French Lieutenant's Woman*, an affectionate parody of a Victorian novel, although one with three different endings to the main love story.

Elizabeth Barrett Browning told the story of her love for Robert Browning in *Sonnets from the Portuguese* –which contained 'How Do I Love Thee?' The title of the sequence was chosen partly to disguise how personal the poems were, by suggesting that they were a translation. But there was an in-joke there too: 'the Portuguese' was Robert's nickname for Elizabeth, because of her dark complexion. The Brownings were forced to marry in secret – because her tyrannical father forbade any of his adult children to marry anyone ever. (Elizabeth was forty at the time.) They then eloped to Italy, where they spent most of their time until her death in 1861. Throughout that time too, she was generally considered a better poet than he was.

In 1992 the second dead heat in Booker Prize history saw *Sacred Hunger* by Barry Unsworth sharing the award with Michael Ondaatje's *The English Patient*, which went on to achieve another historic second – as a Booker winner that became a film which went on to win the Oscar for Best Picture. The only previous example was *Schindler's Ark* by Thomas Keneally, filmed by Steven Spielberg under its American title of *Schindler's List*.

# Round Five

## Literary Festival: a Christmas Round

1. Turkey
2. Holly Golightly
3. *Hangover Square*
4. *Mary Barton*
5. Rudolf Steiner
6. Carol Shields
7. *Where Angels Fear to Tread*
8. *The Vicar of Wakefield*
9. *Summoned by Bells*
10. 'The Star-Spangled Banner', written in 1814 and later to become the American national anthem – although only in 1916. F. Scott Fitzgerald (full forenames Francis Scott Key) was named after the poet, who was a distant relative of his father's.

# Quiz Two

# Round One

## Literary Twosomes, Couples and Double Acts

Q2

1 Who wrote *1066 and All That*?

2 Which fictional pair are introduced by the author as follows: 'They were standing under a tree, each with an arm around the other's neck' – the author in question being Lewis Carroll?

3 Who wrote the 1965 play *The Odd Couple*?

4 As whom are Proteus and Valentine better known in a play of the 1590s?

5 Whose crime novels include *Knots & Crosses*, *Black & Blue* and *Hide & Seek*?

6 What connects Tom Stoppard with the 1981 winner of the Rear of the Year award?

7 Which couple provide the title for a 1988 novel by Peter Carey?

8 Who were the parents of Mary Shelley, the author of *Frankenstein*?

9 Which two poets published *Lyrical Ballads* in 1798?

10 Whose first novel, in 1939, was called *At Swim-Two-Birds*?



Answers on p. 47

# Round Two

## Carry On Reading: Double Entendre in Classic Literature

Q2

For the following passages, please identify the book and author responsible for these unintentional moments of what some purists might consider to be cheap comedy. In all cases, the proper nouns should be a clue.

1 A kindly bachelor, and organist, falls in love in a novel of 1844:

It must be acknowledged that, asleep or awake, Tom's position in reference to this young lady was full of uneasiness. The more he saw of her, the more he admired her beauty, her intelligence, the amiable qualities that even won on the divided house of Pecksniff, and in a few days restored at all events the semblance of harmony and kindness between the two angry sisters. When she spoke, Tom held his breath, so eagerly he listened; when she sang, he sat like one entranced. She touched his organ, and from that bright epoch, even it, the old companion of his happiest hours, incapable as he had thought of elevation, began a new and deified existence.

2 From a chapter called 'Enter the Aunts and Uncles' in a novel of 1860:

The Dodsons were certainly a handsome family, and Mrs Glegg was not the least handsome of the


Answers on p. 49

sisters. As she sat in Mrs Tulliver's arm-chair, no impartial observer could have denied that for a woman of fifty she had a very comely face and figure, though Tom and Maggie considered their aunt Glegg as the type of ugliness. It is true she despised the advantages of costume, for though, as she often observed, no woman had better clothes, it was not her way to wear her new things out before her old ones. Mrs Glegg had doubtless the glossiest and crispest brown curls in her drawers, as well as curls in various degrees of fuzzy laxness.

3 From a novel of 1847:

This lane inclined uphill all the way to Hay; having reached the middle, I sat down on a stile which led thence into a field. Gathering my mantle about me, and sheltering my hands in my muff, I did not feel the cold, though it froze keenly; as was attested by a sheet of ice covering the causeway, where a little brooklet, now congealed, had overflowed after a rapid thaw some days since. From my seat I could look down on Thornfield: the grey and battlemented hall was the principal object in the vale below me.

4 From a novel of 1816:

Mrs Goddard was the mistress of a School – not of a seminary, or an establishment, or any thing which professed, in long sentences of refined nonsense, to combine liberal acquirements with elegant morality upon new principles and new systems – and where young ladies for enormous pay might be screwed

Answers on p. 49

out of health and into vanity – but a real, honest, old-fashioned Boarding-school.

(Clue: One of the pupils at Mrs Goddard's school is called Harriet Smith)



5 The lovers get together at last – in a literary heavy-weight's second novel in 1872, whose title is a quotation from Shakespeare's *As You Like It*:

Here, upon the bright after-glow about the horizon, was now visible an irregular shape, which at first he conceived to be a bough standing a little beyond the line of its neighbours. Then it seemed to move, and, as he advanced still further, there was no doubt that it was a living being sitting in the bank, head bowed on hand. The grassy margin entirely prevented his footsteps from being heard, and it was not till he was close that the figure recognised him. Up it sprang, and he was face to face with Fancy.

'Dick, Dick! O, is it you, Dick!'

'Yes, Fancy,' said Dick in a rather repentant tone, and lowering his nuts.

6 Finally in this round, another early novel by a literary heavyweight, this one from 1876 – and here you even get the first name of the eponymous hero. (He's the one with the beautiful soul.)

Roderick sat staring a moment longer at the floor, then he sprang up and laid his hand affectionately on his friend's shoulder. 'You are the best man in the world,' he said, 'and I am a vile brute. Only,' he added in a moment, 'you don't understand me!' And he looked at him with eyes of such radiant lucidity that



Answers on p. 50

one might have said (and Rowland did almost say so, himself) that it was the fault of one's own grossness if one failed to read to the bottom of that beautiful soul.

Rowland smiled sadly. 'What is it now? Explain.'

'Oh, I can't explain!' cried Roderick impatiently, returning to his work. 'I have only one way of expressing my deepest feelings – it's this!' And he swung his tool.

Answers on p. 50

# Round Three

## Featured Author: P. G. Wodehouse



1 In Wodehouse's name, what do the P. and the G. stand for?

2 What connects Wodehouse and Raymond Chandler educationally?

3 What was significant about the Wodehouse story *Extricating Young Gussie*?

4 What's Jeeves's first name?

5 What's the name of Bertie Wooster's least favourite aunt?

6 Wodehouse collaborated on several musicals with the man who later wrote the musical *Showboat*. Who was he?

7 Who or what is the Empress of Blandings?

8 What did Wodehouse do in the summer of 1941 that dramatically affected the rest of his life?

9 What's the profession of Sir Roderick Glossop?

10 Complete this quotation from *Blandings Castle and Elsewhere*: 'It is never difficult to distinguish between a Scotsman with a grievance and . . .'



Answers on p. 51

# Round Four

## A Round on the Links: Literary Connections

Q2

Can you link the following literary people or things?

1 Tommy Beresford's crime-solving partner in several Agatha Christie novels and short stories

Somerset Maugham writes about Tahiti

The first novel in Paul Scott's *Raj Quartet*

*The Pisan Cantos*

2 Alex and his droogs speaking Nadsat

Lawrence Durrell in Cyprus

The Joad family flee the Oklahoma dustbowl of the 1930s

What his friends called P. G. Wodehouse

3 *Waterland*

*Beau Geste*

'Hail to thee, blithe Spirit'

Iain Banks's 1992 road

4 In 1985 Oliver Sacks has one of the few bestsellers in literary history about neurology

John le Carré's tailor



Answers on pp. 53–5

The Scottish farmer whose horse loses her tail to a witch in a poem by Robert Burns

What seems from all available statistics to have been the best-selling novel of the nineteenth century

Answers on p. 55

# Round Five

## One After the Other: an Alphabetical Round



All the answers here consist of two words, which in each case begin with consecutive letters of the alphabet.

1 What's the third in Louisa M. Alcott's series of novels about the March sisters?

2 What's the actual name (i.e. not the nickname) of the most famous literary creation of Leslie Charteris?

3 Who wrote the *Clayhanger* series of novels, set in his native Potteries?

4 Whose first two novels were *Hideous Kinky* and *Peerless Flats*?

5 Whose last two novels were *The Years* and *Between the Acts*?

6 Which Turkish writer won the Nobel Prize for Literature in 2006?

7 *Frederica*, *Venetia* and *The Black Sheep* are among whose Regency romances – a genre she's generally credited with inventing?

8 Whose plays include *The Wild Duck* and *Hedda Gabler*?

9 Which Scottish writer's novels include *A Disaffection* and *How Late it Was, How Late*?


Answers on p. 57

10 Who, by the time of her death in 2000, had apparently written 723 novels?

Answers on p. 57

# Quiz Two: Answers

## Round One

### Literary Twosomes, Couples and Double Acts

A2

1 W. C. Sellar and R. J. Yeatman

2 Tweedledum and Tweedledee in *Through the Looking Glass*

3 Neil Simon

4 The Two Gentlemen of Verona, in Shakespeare's play

5 Ian Rankin

6 The award went to Felicity Kendal – the leading lady in several of Stoppard's plays, and for many years in his own life too.

7 Oscar and Lucinda

8 William Godwin and Mary Wollstonecraft – respectively, the radical philosopher and the author of *A Vindication of the Rights of Woman*. Wollstonecraft died of a fever ten days after Mary's birth.

9 William Wordsworth and Samuel Taylor Coleridge

10 Flann O'Brien

# Round Two

## Carry On Reading: Double Entendre in Classic Literature

A2

1 From *Martin Chuzzlewit* by Charles Dickens. Tom Pinch is the trusting assistant of the hypocritical Mr Pecksniff, and the woman touching his organ is Mary Graham, Martin's fiancée. Still, at least Martin proves sympathetic to his friend's plight. He promises that when he and Mary are married, they'll build Tom a music room to play his organ in: 'There you shall play away, Tom, till you tire yourself; and, as you like to do so in the dark, it shall *be* dark; and many's the summer evening Mary and I will sit and listen to you, Tom; be sure of that!'

2 From *The Mill on the Floss* by George Eliot. Eliot is, naturally, referring to Mrs Glegg's habit of not wearing the wigs she kept at home in drawers.

3 From *Jane Eyre* by Charlotte Brontë, with Jane taking a walk from Thornfield Hall where she's become the governess to Mr Rochester's ward, Adèle Varens. At this stage, she still hasn't met the man himself, but it's while on this walk that she meets a handsome stranger whose horse slips on the ice – and who duly turns out to be Mr Rochester.

4 From Jane Austen's *Emma* – where Mrs Goddard's pupil Harriet Smith will later become Emma's pet project

5 From Thomas Hardy's *Under the Greenwood Tree* – with Dick Dewy and Fancy Day finally about to overcome their many misunderstandings. Dick of course had just been out collecting nuts, or as Hardy puts it: 'Never man nutted as Dick nutted that afternoon.'

6 From *Roderick Hudson* by Henry James, the story of a young Massachusetts sculptor and a profoundly serious exploration of the nature of art

# Round Three

## Featured Author: P. G. Wodehouse



1 Pelham Grenville

2 They both went to Dulwich College. Although not there at the same time, they did have the same English teacher.

3 It marked the first appearance of Jeeves and Bertie Wooster.

4 Reginald

5 Aunt Agatha ('who eats broken bottles and wears barbed wire next to the skin')

6 Jerome Kern

7 A pig – or, to be more specific, Lord Emsworth's prize sow in the stories about Blandings Castle

8 Having been taken a prisoner of war by the Germans when they invaded France (where Wodehouse was living in 1940) he made five radio broadcasts from Germany. Despite their innocuous comic tone, Wodehouse was branded by many as a traitor, and after the war he moved to America and never visited Britain again.

9 Psychiatrist – or 'loony doctor' as Bertie Wooster more often puts it

10 '. . . a ray of sunshine.'

# Round Four

## A Round on the Links: Literary Connections

A2

### 1 MONEY – ESPECIALLY THE PRE-DECIMAL KIND

Tommy and Tuppence Beresford are Christie's recurring pair of married sleuths, who also star in her last novel, the somewhat rambling *Postern of Fate*.

Somerset Maugham's novel *The Moon and Sixpence* draws heavily on the life of Paul Gauguin, and so ends up in Tahiti.

Paul Scott began the *Raj Quartet* with *The Jewel in the Crown* – as in (for younger quizzers) five shillings. *The Jewel in the Crown* was also the title of Granada Television's adaptation of the quartet, back in the days when ITV made sixteen-hour versions of literary works.

*The Pisan Cantos* are by Ezra Pound, written while he was under arrest by the Americans for his pro-fascist wartime broadcasts from Italy, and possibly while he was mentally ill.

### 2 FRUIT

Nadsat is the dialect spoken by Alex and his teenage gang (known as the droogs) in *A Clockwork Orange* by Anthony Burgess. The language draws heavily on Russian, with *nadsat* itself the Russian for teenager, and *droog* the Russian for friend.

Lawrence Durrell's travel book about Cyprus was called *Bitter Lemons*. The book is set in the village of Bellapais, which Durrell described as a 'haven of rest and paradise of peace' – a description that's now used to attract holiday-makers to its many restaurants and gift-shops.

The Joad family flee from that Oklahoma dustbowl to California in John Steinbeck's *The Grapes of Wrath*.

As established in the last round, the P. in P. G. Wodehouse's name stands for Pelham – which is why he was known to family and friends as 'Plum'. It's also why a late collection of his stories and journalism was called *Plum Pie*.

3 BIRDS

*Waterland* is the 1983 novel by Graham Swift set in the Fens.

*Beau Geste* is a much-filmed novel by P. C. Wren, set in the French Foreign Legion.

'Hail to thee' etc. is the first line of Percy Bysshe Shelley's 'To a Skylark'.

Iain Banks's 1992 novel was *The Crow Road*, which has one of the more striking first lines in literature: 'It was the day my grandmother exploded.'

4 HATS

Oliver Sacks is the neurologist whose bestselling collections of case studies include 1985's *The Man who Mistook His Wife for a Hat*. (His other big hit was *Awakenings*, which became a movie starring Robert de Niro and Robin Williams.)



John le Carré wrote *The Tailor of Panama*.

The Scottish farmer was Tam o'Shanter in the poem by Burns, which influenced the language in more ways than that one. Not only did the Tam o'Shanter hat get its name from the protagonist, but a famous ship was also named after the witch's shirt in the poem: a cutty-sark. Near the beginning, Burns refers to 'Auld Ayr, wham ne'er a town surpasses,/ For honest men and bonny lasses' – which is why Ayr United FC have the nickname of 'The Honest Men'.

The best-selling novel of the nineteenth century (and presumably of all time until then) is generally thought to have been *Trilby* by George Du Maurier, Daphne's granddad. Published in 1894, his tale of how the eponymous artist's model becomes a singing star remained a sensation for many years. Although it's not read so much these days, several of its phrases are, like those of 'Tam o'Shanter', still around. The trilby itself got its name from the type of headgear the heroine wore in Beerbohm Tree's stage version; her mysterious mentor is called Svengali; and her preferred euphemism for posing nude is 'in the altogether'. *Trilby* was such a huge hit in America too that a town in Florida was named after it.

# Round Five

## One after the Other: [illegible]

[illegible] – the first two [illegible]

[illegible]

[illegible] Beauty [illegible]

[illegible] Freud [illegible]

[illegible]

[illegible] Ibsen [illegible]

[illegible]

## Round Five

### One After the Other: an Alphabetical Round

A2

1. *Little Men* – the first two being *Little Women* and *Good Wives* (now often published together)
2. Simon Templar – aka The Saint
3. Arnold Bennett
4. Esther Freud
5. Virginia Woolf
6. Orhan Pamuk
7. Georgette Heyer
8. Henrik Ibsen
9. James Kelman
10. Barbara Cartland, who in her heyday was producing a book a fortnight

# Quiz Three

# Round One

## World of Books: Literary Globetrotting



1 Which novel opens with Raskolnikov walking out into the streets of St Petersburg?

2 Which literary hero lives in St Petersburg with his Aunt Polly and his half-brother Sid?

3 In which 1990s novel does Quoyle rebuild his life in Newfoundland?

4 In which language did Franz Kafka write?

5 Who, in the 1850s, wrote the highly influential three-volume work of art history *The Stones of Venice*?

6 Who, in the 1950s, wrote the highly influential food books *French Country Cooking* and *Italian Food*?

7 What's the main title of the Bill Bryson book that's subtitled *Travels in Europe*?

8 Which country is the setting for *Things Fall Apart* by Chinua Achebe?

9 Who wrote the 2000 romantic novel *Zabibah and the King* – which received rave reviews in all the newspapers in Iraq, became a bestseller there and won the Baghdad Book Club Award?

10 With what sort of fiction would you associate the name Angela Brazil?


Answers on p. 75

# Round Two

## Fact and Fiction

All of the following passages feature real-life people turning up in novels. Please identify the book and author in each case.

Q3

1 I hung around for a while feeling a total git, then spotted Simon from Marketing. When I was almost there, however, I noticed that, unfortunately, Simon from Marketing was talking to Julian Barnes. I hovered indecisively then started to sidle away, at which point Simon said in an irritated superior voice (one you, funnily enough, never hear him use when he is trying to get off with you by the photocopier), 'Did you want something?'

'Ah! Yes!' I said, panicking wildly about what it was I could possibly want. Simon and Julian Barnes looked at me expectantly.

'Do you know where the toilets are?' I blurted. Damn. Damn. Why? Why did I say that? I saw a faint smile hover over the thin-but-attractive lips of Julian Barnes.

2 They got a taxi back to Fiona's place. The cabbie was listening to GLR, and the disc jockey was talking about Kurt Cobain; it took Will a while to understand the strange, muted tone in the DJ's voice.

'What's happened to him?' Will asked the cabbie.

'Who?'



Answers on p. 77

'Kurt Cobain.'

'Is he the Nirvana geezer? He shot himself in the head. Boom.'

'Dead?'

'No. Just a headache. Yeah, course he's dead.'

Will wasn't surprised, particularly, and he was too old to be shocked. He hadn't been shocked by the death of a pop star since Marvin Gaye died. He had been . . . how old? The first of April 1984 . . . Jesus, ten years ago. So he had been twenty-six, and still of an age when things like that meant something.

'Isn't he the singer Marcus liked?' Fiona asked him.

3 This is from a later instalment of the fictional series which made its author the bestselling novelist of the 1980s in Britain. And, as a second clue, the title of the book contains the name of a drink suitable to the era being described. The passage is set in the early hours of 2 May 1997, and features the narrator and his teenage sister . . .

I switched on the television and Rosie joined me as I watched the members of the new Labour government at the victory celebrations at the Royal Festival Hall. As they waited for Tony 'n' Cherie to join them, they jiggled their hips and clicked their fingers to the tune of 'Things Can Only Get Better'.

I squirmed with embarrassment. I was reminded of watching my father dancing at Auntie Susan's wedding reception. As soon as the DJ put on the Rolling Stones' 'Brown Sugar', my father leaped to his feet and began strutting around the hall, *à la* Mick Jagger.

Answers on p. 77

As we watched the dancing politicians, Rosie put her fingers down her throat and made loud retching noises. There was a shot of Peter Mandelson clapping his hands in a loose, American kind of way. She said, 'Gross,' and went to bed.

4 From a second novel which has perhaps been overshadowed by the author's first and third – so here's a clue. Her main character in this book, not untypically, is a half-Chinese, half-Jewish north Londoner with a black Jewish girlfriend.

The bell rings! Here we go! And the first thing that happens is that everyone in attendance realizes that the betting has been pointless. As a wise guy once said, wrestling isn't a sport, it's a spectacle, and you can't bet on it any more than you can bet on the outcome of a performance of *Oedipus Rex*. Of course Big Daddy will win! How could it be otherwise? Look at him! He wears a red Babygro, he is ruddy-faced, he is white-haired, he is more *famous*. Not that Giant Haystacks will lose – he will win too, just by playing his part to its fullest. The more of a bastard he is, the more the audience loves it. When he lifts up his arms, roars and throws back his head like a beast – the International Gesture for *You stupid fools, did you expect me to play fair?* – the whole of the Albert Hall rocks and shakes.

5 On the face of it, this is an unlikely TV announcement, as well as one couched in suitably bureaucratic language. But in which bestselling 1990s novel by whom does it make perfect sense?

 Answers on pp. 77–8

In accordance with the long-standing and well-documented desire of the Führer and People of the Greater German Reich to live in peace and security with the countries of the world, and following extensive consultation with our allies in the European Community, the Reich Ministry for Foreign Affairs, on behalf of the Führer, has today issued an invitation to the President of the United States of America to visit the Greater German Reich for personal discussions aimed at promoting greater understanding between our two peoples. This invitation has been accepted. We understand that the American administration has indicated this morning that Herr Kennedy intends to meet the Führer in Berlin in September. Heil Hitler! Long live Germany!

6 Finally in this round, a Booker Prize-winning novel of the early 1990s – where the subject of the PhD is probably the biggest clue.

His father sent him to Downing College in Cambridge to study under F. R. Leavis. Leavis did to Blackadder what he did to serious students: he showed him the terrible, the magnificent importance and urgency of English literature and simultaneously deprived him of any confidence in his own capacity to contribute to, or change it. The young Blackadder wrote poems, imagined Dr Leavis's comments on them, and burned them. He devised an essay style of Spartan brevity, equivocation and impenetrability. He wrote his PhD on *Conscious Argument and Unconscious Bias: a Source of Tension in the Dramatic Poems of Randolph Henry Ash.*

Answers on p. 78

# Round Three

## Featured Author: Thomas Hardy

Q3

1. What was Hardy's first profession?
2. As what is Michael Henchard known in the title of a Hardy novel?
3. Which Hardy novel takes its title from a phrase in Thomas Gray's 'Elegy Written in a Country Church-Yard'?
4. In *Tess of the d'Urbervilles*, where is Tess arrested for the murder of Alec d'Urberville?
5. Which Hardy novel opens on a Saturday in November, with twilight falling over Egdon Heath?
6. How many times was Hardy married?
7. The savage critical reception of which book is generally agreed to be the reason Hardy gave up writing novels?
8. In *Jude the Obscure*, who hangs Jude and Sue's two youngest children?
9. In his later years, what was the geographically significant name of Hardy's dog?
10. What's unusual about Hardy's final resting place?

 Answers on pp. 79–80

# Round Four

## A Round on the Links: Literary Connections

Can you link the following literary people or things?

Q3

1 A novel by Walter Scott that gave its name to a Scottish football club

The Jonathan Coe novel named after a 1975 LP by prog-rock band Hatfield and the North

The missing word from the title of a short story by F. Scott Fitzgerald: 'The — as Big as the Ritz'

The missing word from the first line of a much-mocked poem by William Wordsworth: '—! with which Wilkinson hath tilled his lands'

2 Twenty-seven novels by Walter Scott

The death of George Osborne in *Vanity Fair*

Michael Bond's most famous literary creation

Elizabeth Smart's most famous literary work

3 (This one needs a bit of non-literary knowledge too)

Henry Fielding's novel about a foundling

An Albert Camus novel set in Amsterdam

Harper Lee's heroic recluse

Aldous Huxley's book in praise of psychedelic drugs


Answers on pp. 81–3

4 (A sadly factual one)

*The Rainbow*

*All Quiet on the Western Front*

*The Satanic Verses*

Thomas Carlyle's *The French Revolution* (accidentally)

Answers on pp. 83–4

# Round Five

## No First Names Here: an Initials Round

Q3

All the answers here are writers with two initials instead of a first name – and just to make it easier, over the course of the round, the initials come in alphabetical order . . .

1. Who wrote the poem beginning 'Jonathan Jo/ Has a mouth like an "O"'?
2. Who wrote the 1981 novel *The White Hotel*?
3. Which literary critic's full-length works include *Revaluation* and *The Great Tradition*?
4. Which cult horror author wrote *At the Mountains of Madness*?
5. Who wrote the novel beginning: 'The past is a foreign country: they do things differently there'?
6. Who wrote the thousand-page 1978 novel about nineteenth-century India called *The Far Pavilions*?
7. Whose plays include *One-Way Pendulum* and *A Resounding Tinkle*?
8. Who created the police detective Adam Dalgleish?
9. Sylvia Plath killed herself in a house once lived in by which poet?
10. Which poet received a big posthumous boost to his sales from the film *Four Weddings and a Funeral*?

 Answers on p. 85

# Quiz Three: Answers

# Round One

## World of Books: Literary Globetrotting

A3

1. *Crime and Punishment* by Fyodor Dostoevsky
2. Tom Sawyer – in the books by Mark Twain. (In a cunning twist, this particular St Petersburg is in Missouri, USA.)
3. *The Shipping News* by E. Annie Proulx
4. German – although he was from Prague, his family was German-speaking.
5. John Ruskin
6. Elizabeth David
7. *Neither Here Nor There*
8. Nigeria
9. Saddam Hussein. One Iraqi reviewer hailed it as 'an innovation in the history of novels' and it later became both a twenty-part television series and a musical.
10. Girls' school stories

## Round Two

### Fact and Fiction

A3

1 From *Bridget Jones's Diary* by Helen Fielding, featuring Bridget at a literary party for the launch of *Kafka's Motorbike*. Barnes did appear as a party guest in the film version, but for that incident was replaced by Salman Rushdie, who was felt to be more recognisable to a movie audience. (To his credit, Barnes apparently took the decision pretty well.)

2 From *About a Boy* by Nick Hornby – where Kurt Cobain becomes one of the key shared interests between cool bachelor Will and Fiona's deeply uncool twelve-year-old son Marcus. The novel's title is based on the Nirvana song 'About a Girl'.

3 That was Adrian Mole, aged 30¼, from Sue Townsend's *Adrian Mole: the Cappuccino Years* – which got its title because Townsend, an old left-winger, believed that New Labour had an awful lot of froth but not much coffee. In the book, one of the Blair babes elected that night was the object of Adrian's long-standing crush, Pandora Braithwaite.

4 From *The Autograph Man*, Zadie Smith's equally multicultural follow-up to *White Teeth*. And while her second novel didn't get as many plaudits or awards as her first – or her third, *On Beauty* – it did win the 2003 *Jewish Quarterly* Wingate Literary Prize.

5 From Robert Harris's *Fatherland*, set in 1964, but in a world where Germany had won the war in Europe and the Americans, the war in the Pacific. The novel takes place in the week leading up to Hitler's seventy-fifth birthday – and, almost incidentally in the circumstances, President Kennedy hasn't been assassinated either.

6 From A. S. Byatt's *Possession*, the 1990 Booker winner, in which the fictional Victorian poet Randolph Henry Ash plays a central role. The novel alternates between his story and that of modern academics studying him. After his time at Cambridge, Blackadder becomes an authority on Ash – many of whose poems Byatt invents and puts in the novel.

# Round Three

## Featured Author: Thomas Hardy



1 He was an architect. (Max Gate, the large Dorset house in which he lived from 1887 onwards, was designed by Hardy himself.)

2 The Mayor of Casterbridge

3 *Far from the Madding Crowd*, Hardy's fourth novel – and the first one successful enough to allow him to take up writing full time. (The full lines in Gray are: 'Far from the madding crowd's ignoble strife,/ Their sober wishes never learned to stray.')

4 At Stonehenge

5 *The Return of the Native*. That opening also features in the Monty Python sketch 'Novel Writing from Dorset'. ('Hello, and welcome to Dorchester, where a very good crowd has turned out to watch local boy Thomas Hardy write his new novel . . .')

6 Twice. His first wife, Emma, died in 1912. His second, Florence, was thirty-nine years his junior.

7 *Jude the Obscure* – or, as it was hilariously dubbed by journalists at the time, *Jude the Obscene*. For the last thirty-three years of his life Hardy wrote only poetry.

8 Jude's son – called Jude, but known as 'Old Father Time' – from his relationship with Arabella Donn. In characteristic Hardy fashion, the boy then hangs

himself too, leaving a note containing the explanation: 'Done because we are too menny'.

9 Wessex – as in the semi-fictional version of the West Country, where many of his novels are set.

10 There are two of them. His heart was buried in Stinsford, Dorset. The rest of him is in Westminster Abbey – where his pall-bearers included John Galsworthy, J. M. Barrie, A. E. Housman, Rudyard Kipling, George Bernard Shaw, Prime Minister Stanley Baldwin, and the leader of the opposition, Ramsay MacDonald.

# Round Four

## A Round on the Links: Literary Connections

A3

### 1 SUITS OF CARDS

Scott's *The Heart of Midlothian* is where the football club – more usually known as Hearts – got its name, albeit in a slightly roundabout way. The club emerged from a nineteenth-century Edinburgh dance-hall which had taken its name from Scott's novel.

The title of Coe's novel, and so of that LP by Hatfield and the North, is *The Rotters' Club*, whose main character is a prog-loving teenager in Seventies Birmingham. The band itself was named after the road sign that used to be at the bottom of the M1.

The Fitzgerald short story is 'The Diamond as Big as the Ritz'.

The Wordsworth poem begins: 'Spade! with which Wilkinson hath tilled his lands' – and really is called 'To the Spade of a Friend'. It duly shows up in many of those anthologies of bad poems by respected poets.

### 2 STATIONS

Waverley station in Edinburgh is named after Scott's 'Waverley' novels, twenty-seven in all – and the ones which are felt to be similar in tone and theme to his first novel, called, naturally enough, *Waverley*. The

Scott Memorial is on Princes Street close to the station's entrance.

George dies at the Battle of Waterloo – soon after marrying Amelia, but even sooner after sending Becky Sharp a note asking her to run away with him.

Michael Bond created Paddington Bear, named after the station where the Brown family find him – with, as you may remember, a note attached to his coat reading 'Please look after this bear'. As you may also remember, Paddington had stowed away from Darkest Peru.

Smart's poetic novel *By Grand Central Station I Sat Down and Wept*, based on her relationship with the poet George Barker, didn't make much of a splash when it was first published in 1945. Since then, though, it's been hailed as a classic, becoming particularly popular with ardent young women – and with Morrissey. His lyrics have quoted Smart's novel at least ten times, and the title of the Smiths' album *Louder than Bombs* is also taken from the book.

3 THEY ALL PROVIDED NAMES FOR POP OR ROCK ACTS

Admittedly, Tom Jones took his stage name more from the 1963 film of Fielding's novel than from the novel itself – whose full title was *The History of Tom Jones, a Foundling*. Nonetheless, if Fielding hadn't existed 'It's Not Unusual' would have been sung by Tommy Scott, the first stage name used by Pontypridd's Thomas Woodward.

Camus's *The Fall* gave its name to the Manchester band (or series of bands) led by Mark E. Smith.

Boo Radley is the local recluse who emerges to save Jem and Scout Finch at the end of Lee's *To Kill a Mockingbird*. The Boo Radleys, by contrast, were a Merseyside band who made it big in the 1990s. Incidentally, the black man falsely accused of rape in the novel is called Tom Robinson, but Tom Robinson the singer was given that name by his parents – so doesn't count for this question.

Huxley's *The Doors of Perception*, which took its own title from a line of William Blake's, described his experiments with mescaline – and also gave the Doors their name.

Other literature-inspired band names include Uriah Heep (from the character in Dickens's *David Copperfield*); Mungo Jerry (from one of T. S. Eliot's Practical Cats); and Steely Dan (from a dildo in *The Naked Lunch* by William Burroughs). There's also a couple inspired by *A Clockwork Orange*, as featured in the last connections round: Heaven 17 (from the name of a band in the novel) and Moloko (from a druggy drink that the droogs used quite a lot). More obscurely, *The Velvet Underground* was originally a pulp paperback about sado-masochism by Michael Leigh.

## 4 BURNED BOOKS

On its publication in 1915, D. H. Lawrence's *The Rainbow* was seized by the police, declared obscene and banned. More than a thousand copies were then burned by order of the examining magistrate.

Erich Maria Remarque's anti-war novel *All Quiet on the Western Front* was one of the books publicly burned by the Nazis in 1933 – although in a happy Hollywood ending, Remarque escaped to America and later married the actress Paulette Goddard.

At the height of the *Satanic Verses* controversy, copies of the novel were publicly burned by some Muslim groups.

Finally, in one of literary history's more poignant mishaps, Carlyle lent the only manuscript of the first volume of *The French Revolution* to his friend John Stuart Mill. Mill's housemaid then found it by the fender and used it to light the fire. Rather heroically, after Mill had broken the news, Carlyle told his wife: 'The poor fellow is terribly cut up. We must endeavour to hide from him how serious this business is to us.' In fact, Carlyle was devastated – not least because he'd kept no notes and was broke at the time. It took him six months to rewrite the burned book. 'I seem to myself', he told his journal when he'd finished, 'like a man that had nearly worn the Life out of him, accomplishing – *zero*.'

# Round Five

## No First Names Here: an Initials Round

A3

1 A. A. Milne. (The poem is 'Jonathan Jo', from *When We Were Very Young*.)

2 D. M. Thomas

3 F. R. Leavis (as featured in Round Two)

4 H. P. Lovecraft

5 L. P. Hartley – in *The Go-Between*

6 M. M. Kaye

7 N. F. Simpson

8 P. D. James

9 W. B. Yeats. The house was in Fitzroy Road, London, and her flat occupied the top two floors.

10 W. H. Auden. In the movie, Matthew (John Hannah) reads the poem 'Funeral Blues' – the one beginning 'Stop all the clocks' – over the coffin of his lover Gareth (Simon Callow). The scene caused Auden's sales to soar.

# Quiz Four

# Round One

## It's War!

1. Which 1969 novel contains an account of the Allied bombing of Dresden – the author having been a prisoner of war there at the time of the raid?
2. Who wrote the series of novels set in the Royal Navy during the Napoleonic wars, and featuring Horatio Hornblower?
3. In *The War of the Worlds* by H. G. Wells, where on the Earth do the Martians land?
4. Which non-fiction bestseller, first published in 1993, contains a torture scene set in Iraq's Abu Ghraib prison?
5. Which classic novel of the Second World War begins: 'It was love at first sight'?
6. Which war poet was killed on the Sambre Canal in 1918 – a week before the Armistice?
7. Which writer died in 1586 from the wounds he received in battle near the Dutch town of Zutphen?
8. In which war did Lord Byron die?
9. Who wrote of her experiences as a nurse in the First World War in *Testament of Youth*?
10. In Homer's *Iliad*, who kills Hector?





Answers on p. 103

# Round Two

## A Little Bit of Politics

1 In which bestselling non-fiction book published in 1993 would you find this characteristic passage, complete with a heartwarmingly Yuletide note at the end?

Q4

Tuesday, 17 December [1985]

If I look back on the last three weeks I can see nothing of any moment whatsoever that has happened to me, save that I suffered, absorbed and phlegmily surmounted a filthy cold in the head.

I have made various 'visits', mainly it seems to workshops for the disabled, to please officials and to give the illusion of activity. But all that has happened is that I am that much older and iller, and I have been kept from the company of my loved ones. I have done nothing for my country, and I would guess that (for example) there are more people out of work today than there were a month ago.

Today we had the Department of Employment carol service. As always, ego and 'rights' to an unbelievable degree. I only can properly enjoy carol services if I am having an illicit affair with someone in the congregation. Why is this?

2 In this one, you just need to identify the author.

'Do shut up int'ruptin',' said Henry, 'I'm tryin' to tell you 'bout this general election. There's four sorts of

 Answers on p. 105

people tryin' to get to be rulers. They all want to make things better, but they want to make 'em better in different ways. There's Conservatives an' they want to make things better by keepin' 'em jus' like what they are now. An' there's Lib'rals an' they want to make things better by alterin' 'em jus' a bit, but not so's anyone'd notice. An' there's Socialists, an' they want to make things better by takin' everyone's money off 'em, and there's Communists an' they want to make things better by killin' everyone but themselves.'

'I'm goin' to be one of them,' said Ginger promptly. 'They sound more excitin' than the others.'

3 Now, for quizzers of a certain age, a trip down memory lane to the vanished world of 1970s politics – but in which novel by whom?

He walks on. At the tables, two groups, the Revolutionary Student Alliance and the Radical Student Coordinating Committee, have fallen out over a principle; they are busy throwing two lots of pamphlets, each labelled *Ulster: The Real Solution*, at each other. Howard ignores the altercation; he passes the tables; he goes on into an area of many notice-boards which, just like the tables, advertise much contention, contradiction, concern. There are notices designed to stimulate self-awareness ('Women's Lib Nude Encounter Group') and self-definition ('Gaysoc Elizabethan Evening: With Madrigals'), reform ('Adopt an Elderly Person') and revolution ('Start the Armed Struggle Now?/ Lunchtime Meeting Addressed by Dr Howard Kirk'). The invitations are rich, the temptations many.

Answers on p. 105

4 This is from the first novel in a six-novel sequence published between 1864 and 1880. Who's the writer, and (perhaps not so easy) what's the title of the book – which takes the form of a question. You may also find that this passage reminds you of more recent political history: between approximately 2 May 1997 and 27 June 2007 . . .

Parliament opened that year on the twelfth of February, and Mr Palliser was one of the first members of the Lower House to take his seat. It had been generally asserted through the country, during the last week, that the Chancellor of the Exchequer existed no longer in the inner world of the Cabinet. He had differed, men said, with his friend and chief, the Prime Minister, and was prepared to launch himself into opposition with his small bodyguard of followers, with all his energy and with all his venom.

There is something very pleasant in the close, bosom friendship and bitter, uncompromising animosity of these human gods. If it were so arranged that the same persons were always friends, and the same persons were always enemies, the thing would not be nearly so interesting.



5 Which Nobel Laureate is this speaking on his seventy-fifth birthday, which he celebrated with a visit to the Soviet Union in 1931?

We don't know how to adequately express our gratitude for all that your country's Communist government has done for us. It's a real comfort to me, an old man, to be able to step into my grave with the knowledge that the civilisation of the world will be saved.


Answers on p. 105–6

It is here in Russia that I have actually been convinced that the new Communist system is capable of leading mankind out of its present crisis, and saving it from complete anarchy and ruin.

6 The term opened vigorously as usual. -- -- stood bronzed before her class and said, 'I have spent most of my summer holidays in Italy once more, and I have brought back a great many pictures which we can pin on the wall. Here is a larger formation of Mussolini's fascisti, it is a better view of them than that of last year's picture. They are doing splendid things as I shall tell you later. I went with my friends for an audience with the Pope. I wore a long black gown with a lace mantilla, and looked magnificent. Mussolini is one of the greatest men in the world, far more so than Ramsay MacDonald.

Answers on p. 106

## Round Three

### Featured Author: Enid Blyton

1 Name all five of the Famous Five.

2 In the *Famous Five* books, what's the surname of the children – which is also the surname of Uncle Quentin, the name of his cottage and the name of a nearby island?

Q4

3 Which Blyton character was described in *Encounter* literary magazine in 1958 as 'the most egocentric, joyless, snivelling and pious anti-hero in the history of British fiction'?

4 Complete this remark by Enid Blyton: 'I take no notice of critics . . .'

5 Which series of Blyton books features a dog called Scamper?

6 Enid Blyton wrote more than seven hundred books. To the nearest twenty, how many are written in the first person?

7 Darrell Rivers is the heroine of which six-book series by Blyton?

8 What's the full name of Fatty in the *Five Find-Outers and Dog* series?

9 Blyton wrote eight books about Jack, Philip, Dinah, Lucy-Ann – and Kiki, who, just for a change, was their pet parrot. What are the last two words of the


Answers on p. 107

titles of all eight books?

10 At the time of her death in 1968, Blyton was the third bestselling British writer ever. Which two were above her?

Answers on p. 107

# Round Four

## A Round on the Links: Literary Connections

Can you link the following literary people or things?



1 John Osborne's cross protagonist

The 1959 book that features a Miss Burdock in the title (although she's called there by her first name)

Compton Mackenzie's 1947 novel about a lucky shipwreck

The pen-name of Hector Hugh Munro

2 (A children's book special)

*Stig of the Dump*

The Hans Christian Andersen story in which Gerda rescues Kay

Antoine de Saint-Exupéry

Meg Cabot

3 The villainous Dartmoor resident Jack Stapleton, in 1902

The first book by Charles Darwin

The third novel by Frederick Forsyth, which takes its title from a line in *Julius Caesar*

The best-known literary creation of H. C. McNeile, once of the Royal Engineers – which is significant


Answers on p. 109–11

4 *News from Nowhere*

Twice over, *The Good Soldier*

The poet laureate from 1896 to 1913

The verse form known as the clerihew

Answers on pp. 111–12

# Round Five

## Animal Farm: a Zoological Round

All the answers here contain or comprise the name of an animal.

Q4

1. What kind of animal is Beatrix Potter's Jeremy Fisher?
2. What's the title of the bestselling 1969 book for young children by Eric Carle?
3. Still with children's books, who's the most famous literary creation of Jean de Brunhoff?
4. How is the Greek playwright Aeschylus traditionally said to have died?
5. Which nineteenth-century essayist wrote under the pen-name Elia?
6. Which 1937 novel features the itinerant labourers George and Lennie?
7. What's the only Shakespeare play with an animal in the title?
8. Which Margaret Atwood novel concerns a painter called Elaine Risley returning to Toronto?
9. While she was working in advertising, which long-running advertising bird did Dorothy L. Sayers invent?
10. What's the first novel in Cormac McCarthy's *Border Trilogy*?


Answers on p. 113

# Quiz Four: Answers

## Round One

### It's War!

1 *Slaughterhouse-Five* by Kurt Vonnegut

2 C. S. Forester

3 Woking, Surrey. Not as peculiar as it might seem – because Wells was living in Woking when he wrote the book.

4 *Bravo Two-Zero* by Andy McNab. (In those days the Iraqis were doing the torturing.)

5 *Catch-22* by Joseph Heller. The love is Yossarian's for the Air Force chaplain.

6 Wilfred Owen

7 Sir Philip Sidney – whose friend Fulke Greville is responsible for the story that, as he was being carried from the field, Sidney gave his water bottle to a dying soldier with the words, 'Thy necessity is yet greater than mine.' Greville, sadly, hadn't been there at the time.

8 The Greek War of Independence – although he died of a fever before seeing any serious military action

9 Vera Brittain – Shirley Williams's mum

10 Achilles

# Round Two

## A Little Bit of Politics

A4

1 An entry from Alan Clark's *Diaries* – giving us a typical blend of honesty, self-pity, hypochondria and lechery. The book was dedicated to his wife, 'my beloved Jane, around whose cool and affectionate personality there raged this maelstrom of egocentricity and self-indulgence'.

2 Richmal Crompton on top form in a story called *William Prime Minister*. That political story is normally considered more successful than *William and the Nasties* from 1934, in which the Outlaws plan to drive a Jewish shopkeeper from the village. As you might expect, that story isn't reprinted any more. As you might not, it was only dropped from the collection *William the Detective* in 1986.

3 From Malcolm Bradbury's *The History Man*, set in the far-off days of Seventies campus radicalism – before students, and lecturers, either sold out or wised up according to your political taste. Fortunately for sociology lecturer Howard Kirk, it was also a time when sleeping with your students was regarded less as sexual harassment and more as a perk of the job.

4 That was the Prime Minister and the Chancellor, turning from close allies into sworn enemies in Anthony Trollope's *Can You Forgive Her?*. Over the course of the six novels, Plantagenet Palliser ends up

both Prime Minister and the Duke of Omnium. To pub-quizzers, mind you, Trollope may be equally famous for introducing the pillar box to Britain. (He worked for the Post Office from 1834 until 1867.)

5 That was George Bernard Shaw speaking at Moscow's Trade Union Central Hall – the same hall that his host Stalin would soon be using for show trials. During his trip, as Michael Holroyd's biography explains, Shaw also 'congratulated Soviet citizens engaged in compulsory labour on working for public service and not for the private profit of a few individuals: "I wish we had forced labour in England," he added, "in which case we would not have 2,000,000 unemployed."' Other Soviet celebrations for the great man's birthday included the Bernard Shaw Handicap at a nearby race course – although, for the record, Shaw didn't actually step into his grave for another nineteen years. Stalin, says Holroyd, later complained to his daughter that Shaw was 'an awful person'.

Another of Shaw's great (and equally doomed) causes was spelling reform. After the atom bombs had been dropped on Japan, he wrote to *The Times* to protest – about the unnecessary 'b' on the end of the word 'bomb'.

6 From Muriel Spark's *The Prime of Miss Jean Brodie* – and the start of the autumn term of 1931 at Marcia Blaine School for Girls. Miss Brodie's fascist leanings later get her the sack, when she encourages Joyce Emily to fight for Franco in the Spanish Civil War.

## Round Three

### Featured Author: Enid Blyton

A4

1. Julian, Dick, Anne, George (aka, but not very often, Georgina) and Timmy the dog – although true Blyton fans will know that in the first *Famous Five* book, the dog is called Timothy or Tim
2. Kirrin
3. Noddy
4. '. . . over twelve years of age.'
5. The *Secret Seven* books
6. None. She believed that children don't like first-person narratives.
7. The *Malory Towers* series
8. Frederick Algernon Trotteville
9. 'Of Adventure' – from *The Island of Adventure* (1944) to *The River of Adventure* (1955)
10. Agatha Christie and William Shakespeare

P. S. Anybody who wants to take a more scholarly approach to the works of Enid Blyton – or just to have a cheap laugh at modern academics – should try *Enid Blyton and the Mystery of Children's Literature* (2000) by David Rudd. The chapter titles include 'Noddy: Discursive Threads and Intertextuality' and 'Sexism or

Subversion: Querying Gender Relations in *The Famous Five* and *Malory Towers*'. Rudd also gives us the useful tip that when reading Blyton 'Barthes's notion of "text as a field of force", to which Bergonzi alludes, is a helpful image to bear in mind'.

Still, at least Rudd was trying to rehabilitate Blyton after the pounding she'd received from educational experts over previous decades for her sexism, racism and snobbery. In the 1970s, for instance, she came under particular fire from a group rather optimistically called Librarians for Social Change.

# Round Four

## A Round on the Links: Literary Connections

1 ALCOHOLIC DRINKS

Jimmy Porter (as in stout or Guinness) is the main character in Osborne's *Look Back in Anger*.

A4

Miss Burdock's first name was Rosie – and so the book is *Cider with Rosie* by Laurie Lee.

Compton Mackenzie's *Whisky Galore* features a ship carrying fifty thousand cases of 'the water of life' being wrecked off the Hebrides at the height of wartime rationing. Thanks to the Ealing comedy version, *Whisky Galore* is probably Mackenzie's best-known book now – although he also wrote the *Monarch of the Glen* novels, which became the basis for that cosy Sunday-night series on BBC1. Less famously, in 1957, Mackenzie published *Sublime Tobacco*, a non-fiction book which had the simple aim of proving through careful historical analysis that smoking is 'one of the greatest boons ever conferred upon humanity'.

Munro is better known as the novelist and short-story writer Saki, a name he took from the cup-bearer in one of his favourite poems, the *Rubáiyát of Omar Khayyám*. He was killed in the First World War, for which he'd volunteered despite being well into his forties.

## 2 MEMBERS OF A NUCLEAR ROYAL FAMILY

*Stig of the Dump*, about the friendship between a young boy called Barney and the eponymous caveman, was written by Clive King in 1963. It's twice been adapted for television – by ITV in 1981 and the BBC in 2002.

The Hans Christian Andersen story is *The Snow Queen*.

*The Little Prince* (1943), narrated by an airman stranded in the desert, is the only book for children by Saint-Exupéry – himself a pioneering pilot. It's also one of the few of his that's not about flying – because Saint-Exupéry was a pioneering pilot as well as a writer. He disappeared in 1944, while on a reconnaissance mission to spy on German troop movements, and the wreckage of his plane wasn't found until 2000. The international airport in his home town is now called Lyon-Saint-Exupéry – and before the Euro was introduced in France, he and his own drawing of the little prince were on the fifty-franc note.

Meg Cabot's highly successful series of books for girls is *The Princess Diaries*, the first volume of which appeared in 2000.

## 3 DOGS

Jack Stapleton is the baddie in Arthur Conan Doyle's *The Hound of the Baskervilles*.

In 1839 Charles Darwin's first book was pithily entitled *Journal of Researches into the Geology and*

*Natural History of the Various Countries Visited by HMS* Beagle. Luckily it's published nowadays as just *Voyage of the Beagle*.

Frederick Forsyth's third novel was Dogs *of War*, referring to mercenary soldiers, but also to Mark Antony's line: 'Cry, "Havoc!" and let slip the dogs of war'.



H. C. McNeile took his pseudonym from the nickname of the Royal Engineers, with whom he served in the First World War. He was therefore Sapper, creator of Bulldog Drummond, the private detective who foiled many a plot by dastardly foreigners to take over Britain. The books were massively popular in the 1920s and 30s, but aren't so fashionable these days. In fact, *The Oxford Companion to English Literature* describes Drummond as 'hefty, ugly, xenophobic and apparently brainless'.

4 MAKES OF CAR

Published in 1891, *News from Nowhere* was a utopian Socialist novel by William Morris – now perhaps best known as a wallpaper designer.

*The Good Soldier* (1915) is thought by most people – including himself – to be the best novel by Ford Madox Ford. (Hence twice over.)

Alfred Austin was the poet laureate in question. Nobody would call him the best poet ever to hold the post. (Indeed, plenty of people have called him the worst.) He was, though, certainly patriotic enough – with poems such as 'A Dream of England',

'In Praise of England' and 'Who Would Not Die for England!' Unfortunately, the lines often most quoted from him, about the illness of the Prince of Wales, are apocryphal. Nowhere in his collected works can you find: 'Along the wires the electric message came/ "He is no better, he is much the same."' None of which stopped Austin from being quite sniffy about his predecessor in the job. 'Mr Tennyson is not a great poet,' he wrote, 'not even at the head of poets of the third rank, among whom he must ultimately take his place.'

Clerihews were invented by Edmund Clerihew Bentley in his 1905 collection *Biography for Beginners*. These four-line rhyming epigrams are considered hilariously witty by some, and have been much copied ever since. A typical example goes like this:

> There exists no proof as
> To who shot William Rufus,
> But shooting him would seem
> To have been quite a sound scheme.

# Round Five

## Animal Farm: a Zoological Round



1. A frog
2. *The Very Hungry Caterpillar*
3. Babar the Elephant
4. When an eagle dropped a tortoise on his head – the story being that the bird mistook Aeschylus's bald head for a rock
5. Charles Lamb
6. *Of Mice and Men* by John Steinbeck
7. *The Taming of the Shrew*
8. *Cat's Eye*
9. The Guinness toucan
10. *All the Pretty Horses*

# Quiz Five

## Round One

### Book Bindings: Literature and Marriage

1. Who wrote the bestselling novel *Lucy Sullivan is Getting Married*?
2. In the novels of John Mortimer, how does Rumpole refer to his wife?
3. Which nineteenth-century literary character marries Isabella Linton?
4. In Chaucer's *Canterbury Tales*, how many times had the Wife of Bath been married?
5. Which of these writers had the most marriages: Ernest Hemingway, Norman Mailer or Saul Bellow?
6. Who wrote the 1697 play *The Provok'd Wife* – before going on to be the architect of Castle Howard and Blenheim Palace?
7. In which novel does the main character marry Charlotte Haze – but only so as to be close to her daughter Dolores?
8. Whose best-ever selling novel was his 1968 book *Couples* – one of his many depictions of suburban adultery?
9. Whose first novel was *The World Is Full of Married Men*?
10. Who depicted a particularly poisonous marriage in his play *The Dance of Death*?





Answers on p. 131

# Round Two

## How Do You Do: First Appearances of Famous Characters

The following passages all contain the moment when what proved to be an unforgettable new literary creation was introduced to the world. In all cases, please identify the character, the book and the author. This round also divides neatly into three villains, followed by three sex-pots. (And, just to get you started, for the first villain you should note his keen interest in food.)

Q5

1 Steel bars covered the entire front of the cell. Behind the bars, farther than arm's reach, was a stout nylon net stretched ceiling to floor and wall to wall. Through the barrier, Graham could see a table and chair bolted to the floor.

The man lay on his cot asleep. His head propped on a pillow against the wall. Alexandre Dumas's *Le Grand Dictionnaire de Cuisine* was open on his chest.

Graham had stared through the bars for about five seconds when the man opened his eyes and said, 'That's some atrocious aftershave you wore in court.'

The man's eyes are maroon and they reflect the light redly in tiny points. Graham felt each hair bristle on his nape.

2 At that moment, the peace was shattered by an extremely strident motor horn. A large car was coming towards them. It drew up at a big house just

 Answers on p. 133

ahead of them and a tall woman came out on to the front-door steps. She was wearing a tight-fitting emerald satin dress, several ropes of rubies, and an absolutely simple white mink cloak, which reached to the high heels of her ruby-red shoes. She had a dark skin, black eyes with a tinge of red in them, and a very pointed nose. Her hair was parted severely down the middle and one half of it was black and the other white – rather unusual.

3 I heard a heavy step approaching behind the great door, and saw through the chinks the gleam of a coming light. Then there was the sound of rattling chains and the clanking of massive bolts drawn back. A key was turned with the loud grating noise of long disuse, and the great door swung back.

Within stood a tall old man, clean shaven save for a long white moustache, and clad in black from head to foot, without a single speck of colour about him anywhere. He motioned me in with his right hand with a courtly gesture, saying in excellent English, but with a strange intonation:–

'Welcome to my house! Enter freely and of your own will!'

And so to the first appearances of the sexy characters, beginning with this heroine, who's about to be embarrassed by her old dad . . .

4 She was a fine and handsome girl – not handsomer than some others, possibly – but her mobile peony mouth and large innocent eyes added eloquence to colour and shape. She wore a red ribbon in her hair,

Answers on pp. 133–4

and was the only one of the company who could boast of such a pronounced adornment. As she looked round her father was seen moving along the road in a chaise belonging to the Pure Drop Inn, driven by a frizzle-haired brawny damsel. Leaning back, and with his eyes closed luxuriously, he was waving his hand above his head, and singing in a slow recitative –

'I've-got-a-gr't-family-vault-at-Kingsbere – and knighted-forefathers-in-lead-coffins-there!'

5 Here, in translation, two people meet who will later become lovers. But who's the woman with the impressive eyelashes – and whose name is also the title of the novel? One final clue: the location of the meeting turns out to be ironically significant . . .

Q5

He followed the guard to the carriage, and at the door of the compartment had to stop and make way for a lady who was getting out. His experience as a man of the world told him at a glance that she belonged to the best society. He begged her pardon and was about to enter the carriage but felt he must have another look at her – not on account of the elegance and unassuming grace of her whole figure, but because of something tender and caressing in her lovely face as she passed him. As he looked round, she too turned her head. Her brilliant grey eyes, shadowed by thick lashes, gave him a friendly, attentive look. In that brief glance he had time to notice the suppressed animation which played over her face and flitted between her sparkling eyes and the slight smile curving her red lips.

 Answers on p. 134

6 Finally in this round, here's a sexpot for the ladies – from a novel that became a (posthumously) huge bestseller for a very specific reason.

She was watching a brown spaniel that had run out of a side-path, and was looking towards them with lifted nose, making a soft, fluffy bark. A man with a gun strode swiftly, softly out after the dog, facing their way as if about to attack them; then stopped instead, saluted, and was turning downhill. He had frightened her, he seemed to emerge with such a swift menace. That was how she had seen him, like the sudden rush of a threat out of nowhere.

He was a man in dark green velveteens and gaiters . . . the old style, with a red face and red moustache and distant eyes. He was moderately tall and lean, and was silent. He did not look at her at all, only at the chair.

Answers on p. 134

# Round Three

## Featured Author: John le Carré

1 What connects le Carré with the 1970s TV series *Rock Follies*, starring Julie Covington, Rula Lenska and Charlotte Cornwell?

2 Le Carré's breakthrough novel was his third, published in 1963. What was it called?

3 How does the title of a 1971 le Carré novel refer to its main character, Aldo Cassidy? (The novel wasn't a spy book and – possibly as a result – was a serious commercial flop.)

4 'The best English novel since the war' was Philip Roth's verdict on which le Carré book – according to le Carré himself, his most autobiographical?

5 *Smiley's People* was the third book in a trilogy that began with which novel?

6 Which country is the main setting for le Carré's *The Constant Gardener*?

7 What's the first name of George Smiley's unfaithful wife?

8 Why were le Carré and his wife in central London on 15 February 2003?

9 Who did le Carré once say was motivated only by 'the self-hate of a vain misfit for whom nothing will ever be worthy of his loyalty'?

 Answers on pp. 135–6

10 In *Tinker, Tailor, Soldier, Spy*, what's the code name for the mole?

Answers on p. 136

# Round Four

## A Round on the Links: Literary Connections

Can you link the following literary people or things?

1 The best-known story in Annie Proulx's *Close Range: Wyoming Stories*

Thomas Mann's Hans Castorp

Inman returns from the American Civil War in Charles Frazier's first novel

William Blake's feet in ancient time

Q5

2 'The Road Not Taken' (a poem)

*Strangers and Brothers* (an eleven-novel sequence)

The man who circled the globe in approximately 115,200 minutes (with a small spelling change)

Richard Hughes's novel of Jamaica

3 *The Big Sleep*

Holden Caulfield's sister in *The Catcher in the Rye*

With Edith Somerville, the co-creator of the Irish RM

A Daphne du Maurier novel of 1951

4 (Professionally speaking)

Mao Tse-tung

 Answers on pp. 137–9

Giacomo Casanova

Philip Larkin

Jorge Luis Borges

Answers on p. 139

# Round Five

## The Rainbow: a Colourful Round

All the answers here contain the name of a colour

1. Who wrote the children's books *Charlotte's Web* and *Stuart Little*?
2. Which enduring classic of 1857 was written by Thomas Hughes?
3. As whom is Anne Shirley better known in a 1908 novel by L. M. Montgomery?
4. In which 1983 novel does the narrator Celie tell of her love for Shug Avery?
5. In which nineteenth-century American classic is the main character Hester Prynne?
6. In which nineteenth-century American classic is the main character Henry Fleming, a Civil War soldier?
7. Name any Iris Murdoch novel with a colour in the title.
8. Which book of 1877 is described on the title page as having been 'translated from the original equine'?
9. In the poem by Edward Lear, in what kind of vessel do the owl and the pussycat go to sea?
10. In the William books of Richmal Crompton, which little girl can 'thcream and thcream' until she's sick?



Answers on p. 141

# Quiz Five: Answers

# Round One

## Book Bindings: Literature and Marriage

1. Marian Keyes
2. She Who Must Be Obeyed
3. Heathcliff – in *Wuthering Heights* by Emily Brontë
4. Five – and her husbands are all dead. ('The first three men were good, and rich, and old'.)
5. Norman Mailer – with six. Bellow was married five times, and Hemingway four.
6. John Vanbrugh
7. *Lolita* by Vladimir Nabokov. (Dolores is known as Lolita for short.)
8. John Updike
9. Jackie Collins
10. August Strindberg

# Round Two

## How Do You Do: First Appearances of Famous Characters

A5

1. The first appearance of Dr Hannibal Lecter, in *Red Dragon* by Thomas Harris. Lecter is a relatively minor character in that book – but went on to play a much bigger role in Harris's later novels, *The Silence of the Lambs*, *Hannibal* and *Hannibal Rising*. He's also, surely, one of the few people in the whole of fiction with maroon eyes.

2. That was Mr and Mrs Dearly looking on as Cruella de Vil comes out to meet her chauffeur in Dodie Smith's *The Hundred and One Dalmatians*. In the next paragraph, Mrs Dearly gives her husband some alarming background information. 'Why, that's Cruella de Vil,' she says. 'We were at school together. She was expelled for drinking ink.'

3. The big entrance of Count Dracula, in Bram Stoker's *Dracula* – with Jonathan Harker becoming the first person ever to hear the heavy footsteps coming towards that Transylvanian castle door and all those bolts being drawn back. In fact, many of the characteristics of the movie *Dracula* were already present and correct in the original novel – apart from that long white moustache. And two pages later, after a nice supper, the Count really does hear some wolves and say, 'The children of the night. What music they make!'

4 Thomas Hardy introducing us to Tess of the d'Urbervilles – or simple Tess Durbeyfield as she is then. Her father's head has just been turned by discovering he is related to the great d'Urberville family of Kingsbere – which sort of leads to Tess being seduced, giving birth to an illegitimate baby who dies, stabbing her lover, being hanged for the crime and so on.

5 Vronsky bumping into Anna Karenina in Leo Tolstoy's novel. First seen on a train, Anna ends up throwing herself under one.

6 From *Lady Chatterley's Lover* by D. H. Lawrence. Lady Constance Chatterley is walking with her wheelchair-bound husband when they meet the new gamekeeper, one Oliver Mellors. After the 1960 trial freed Penguin to publish the unexpurgated version of the novel, it sold two hundred thousand copies on the first day – and around two million more in the next six weeks.

## Round Three

### Featured Author: John le Carré

1 Charlotte Cornwell is le Carré's sister, his real name being David Cornwell (which that question was a somewhat convoluted way of establishing).

2 *The Spy Who Came in from the Cold*

3 *The Naïve and Sentimental Lover*

4 *A Perfect Spy*

5 *Tinker, Tailor, Soldier, Spy*. (The second was *The Honourable Schoolboy*.)

6 Kenya

7 Ann

8 They were at the demonstration against the Iraq war. Just before the war began, le Carré also wrote an essay starkly entitled *The United States Has Gone Mad*. ('How Bush and his junta succeeded in deflecting America's anger from bin Laden to Saddam Hussein is one of the great public relations conjuring tricks of history,' he wrote.)

9 Kim Philby. Actually this is one of his milder remarks about Philby – who, according to some sources, was responsible for ending le Carré's own career in the British secret service by revealing to the Russians that he was a spy. Either way, in 2000, le Carré explained that Philby had 'carried to the

grave my unqualified contempt'.

10 Gerald. The mole (whose real name can't possibly be divulged here) was largely based on Philby.

# Round Four

## A Round on the Links: Literary Connections

1 MOUNTAINS

Despite the fact that the other tales have such memorable titles as 'The Half-Skinned Steer', '55 Miles to the Gas Pump' and 'People in Hell Just Want a Drink of Water', the most famous story in *Close Range* has got to be 'Brokeback Mountain' – about, as you may know, the love between two cowboys.

A5

Hans Castorp is the main character in Mann's *The Magic Mountain*, set in a sanatorium in the Swiss Alps.

Inman, whose first name we never learn, is the protagonist of Frazier's *Cold Mountain* (1997).

'And did those feet in ancient time/ Walk upon England's mountains green?' – from the Preface to Blake's long poem 'Milton', and specifically from the part of the Preface now known as 'Jerusalem'.

2 BAD WEATHER (OR, ALTERNATIVELY, HAZARDOUS DRIVING CONDITIONS)

'The Road Not Taken' is the poem by Robert <u>Frost</u> that contains the lines, 'I took the one less travelled by,/ And that has made all the difference'.

*Strangers and Brothers* is by C. P. <u>Snow</u>. The ninth novel in the series, by the way, is *Corridors of Power*, a phrase Snow had coined in the sixth, *Homecomings* – and which had already caught on. (In the Foreword to *Corridors of Power* he expresses the hope that he's entitled to use his own cliché.)

Phileas Fogg is the main character in Jules Verne's *Around the World in Eighty Days*, whose title was so cunningly disguised there. Incidentally, Fogg never travels by hot-air balloon in the novel. Still, the fact that he briefly considers it at one point was good enough for Hollywood – which is why most people (especially the advertisers of hot-air balloon trips) tend to imagine that he did.

With its unsentimental view of a group of unsupervised children, Richard Hughes's 1929 novel *A High Wind in Jamaica* is sometimes said to prefigure *Lord of the Flies*. The 1965 film version featured an appearance from the young Martin Amis, who by his own account, 'talentlessly played one of the children'. In the finished movie, his voice was dubbed by an elderly woman.

3 CHARACTERS IN THE SITCOM *FRIENDS*

*The Big Sleep* is by Raymond Chandler.

Phoebe is Holden Caulfield's much-loved little sister in J. D. Salinger's novel, and about the only person he regards as not a phoney.

Martin Ross and her second cousin Edith Somerville wrote the highly successful series of stories about the Irish RM, or resident magistrate. (So yes, Martin Ross was a woman.)

And talking of cousins, that 1951 Daphne du Maurier novel was *My Cousin* <u>*Rachel*</u>.

## 4 THEY WERE ALL LIBRARIANS

As a young graduate, Mao worked in a university library, and qualifies as a writer because his *Little Red Book* is one of the bestselling books ever. Its sales were helped by the fact that it was compulsory for every Chinese citizen to own a copy and to carry it at all times.

Casanova anticlimactically spent the last thirteen years of his life as a librarian in what's now the Czech Republic – which is when and where he wrote his scandalous autobiography.

A5

Larkin was a librarian for the whole of his working life, ending up at Hull University.

Borges, who generally appears in all those lists of writers who should have won the Nobel Prize, was first a municipal librarian and eventually the Director of the National Library in Buenos Aires. He resigned when Juan Perón was re-elected President of Argentina in 1973.

(In an interview for the *Paris Review*, Larkin was once asked: 'Is Jorge Luis Borges the only other contemporary poet of note who is also a librarian?' Larkin's reply, inevitably, was, 'Who is Jorge Luis Borges?')

# Round Five

## The Rainbow: a Colourful Round



1 E. B. White

2 *Tom Brown's Schooldays*

3 Anne of Green Gables

4 *The Color Purple* by Alice Walker

5 *The Scarlet Letter* by Nathaniel Hawthorne. Hester is forced by her New England puritan community to wear the scarlet letter itself: an A for adultery.

6 *The Red Badge of Courage* by Stephen Crane

7 *The Black Prince*; *The Green Knight*; *The Red and the Green*. (*An Unofficial Rose* would also be just about acceptable.)

8 *Black Beauty* by Anna Sewell

9 A beautiful pea-green boat

10 Violet Elizabeth Bott

# Quiz Six

## Round One

### Devouring Books: Literary Food and Drink

1 Who wrote the poem containing the phrase, 'Sandalwood, cedarwood and sweet white wine'?

2 Who wrote the play about National Service in the RAF, *Chips with Everything*?

3 In George Orwell's *Nineteen Eighty-Four*, how is the nightmare totalitarian future reflected in the way beer is served?

4 Who caused something of a stir with the frankness of her 1962 feminist novel *The Pumpkin Eater*?

Q6

5 Who wrote the dramatic monologue, originally for television, *A Cream Cracker under the Settee*?

6 In which comic classic is a picnic ruined because the participants have forgotten a tin-opener?

7 Who wrote *The Life and Opinions of Tristram Shandy*?

8 A taste of which foodstuff prompted the original Proustian rush?

9 According to his own doctor, which French novelist, author of *Le Père Goriot* and *Le Cousin Pons*, died of caffeine poisoning?

10 What's the connection between coffee and Captain Ahab's first mate in *Moby-Dick*?


Answers on p. 159

# Round Two

## Dear Sir or Madam: Literature and Letters

1 The person who wrote this 1893 letter must later have come to regret that he did. Who's he, and who's he writing to?

My Own Boy,

Your sonnet is quite lovely, and it is a marvel that those red rose-leaf lips of yours should have been made no less for music of song than for madness of kisses. Your slim gilt soul walks between passion and poetry. I know Hyacinthus, whom Apollo loved so madly, was you in Greek days.

Come here whenever you like. It is a lovely place – it only lacks you.

Always, with undying love, yours . . .



2 In this extraordinarily sad letter from 1848, can you name both the writer and the person being written about? For the writer, you may find yourself torn in three directions – but the (admittedly tough) clue is meant to be the phrase 'a year my junior'.

My Dear Sir

A lull begins to succeed the gloomy tumult of last week. It is not permitted us to grieve for him who is gone as others grieve for those they lose. I do not weep from a sense of bereavement – there is no prop withdrawn, no consolation torn away, no dear companion lost – but for the wreck of talent, the ruin



Answers on p. 161

of promise, the untimely dreary extinction of what might have been a burning and a shining light. My brother was a year my junior. I had aspirations and ambitions for him once, long ago – they have perished mournfully. Nothing remains of him but a memory of errors and sufferings.

My unhappy brother never knew what his sisters had done in literature – he was never aware that they had ever published a line. We could not tell him of our own efforts for fear of causing him too deep a pang of remorse for his own time misspent, and talents misapplied. Now he will never know.

3 This 1812 letter put a crunching end to one of literary history's most notoriously tempestuous love affairs – and also contains a savage twist to the traditional line about hoping to stay friends. Who wrote the letter, and who was its unfortunate recipient?

My dear lady

I am no longer your lover; and since you oblige me to confess it by this truly unfeminine persecution, learn that I am attached to another, whose name it would of course be dishonourable to mention. I shall ever remember with gratitude the many instances I have received of the predilection you have shown in my favour. I shall ever continue your friend, if your ladyship will permit me so to style myself; and as proof of my regard, I offer you this advice: correct your vanity, which is ridiculous; exert your absurd caprices upon others; and leave me in peace.

Answers on p. 161

4 Here's a fairly ungallant description of a major female writer – from an 1869 letter by a young American who'd just visited her. Later he'd become as famous a novelist as she was, and settle permanently in England. Please name them both.

She is magnificently ugly – deliciously hideous. She has a low forehead, a dull grey eye, a vast pendulous nose, a huge mouth full of uneven teeth and a chin and jawbone *qui n'en finissent pas*. In this vast ugliness resides a most powerful beauty which, in a very few minutes, steals forth and charms the mind, so that you end as I ended, in falling in love with her. Yes behold me literally in love with this great horse-faced blue-stocking. Altogether, she has a larger circumference than any woman I have ever seen.



5 On to the twenty-first century now, from the first part of an open letter to the American president from someone perhaps better known as a film-maker. Book and author please.

I would like to ask you three pointed questions – and I would like you to give me, and the American people, three honest answers:

1. George, are you able to read and write on an adult level?

It appears to me and many others that, sadly, you may be a functional illiterate. This is nothing to be ashamed of. Millions of Americans cannot read and write above a fourth-grade level. But if you have trouble comprehending the complex position papers you are handed as the Leader of Mostly-Free World, how


Answers on p. 162

can we entrust something like our nuclear secrets to you?

All the signs of illiteracy are there. The first clue was what you named as your favourite childhood book. '*The Very Hungry Caterpillar*,' you said.

Unfortunately, that book wasn't even published until a year after you graduated from college.

6 Finally, from 1925, a letter from one American literary giant to another that sums them both up nicely. Who are they?

I'm feeling better than I've ever felt – haven't drunk anything but wine since I left Paris. I wonder what your idea of heaven would be – A beautiful vacuum filled with wealthy monogamists, all powerful and members of the best families, all drinking themselves to death.

To me heaven would be a big bull ring with me holding two barrera seats and a trout stream outside that no one else was allowed to fish in and two lovely houses in the town: one where I would have my wife and children and be monogamous and love them truly and well, and the other where I would have my nine beautiful mistresses on 9 different floors.

Answers on p. 162

## Round Three

### Featured Author: John Keats

1 What's the celebrated first line of Keats's longest poem, 'Endymion'?

2 What's the third word of the poem 'To Autumn'?

3 Within two inches either way, how tall was the adult Keats?

4 In perhaps his worst early poem, to whom is Keats referring in these lines?

> God! She is like a milk-white lamb that bleats
> For man's protection

5 Where did Keats write 'Ode to a Nightingale'?

6 In 1819, who became Keats's fiancée?

7 Which poem contains the line, 'And no birds sing'?

8 How old was Keats when he died?

9 What phrase was written, at his own request, on Keats's tombstone in Rome?

10 What was the title of Percy Bysshe Shelley's fifty-five-stanza elegy on Keats, published in 1821?



 Answers on pp. 163–4

# Round Four

## A Round on the Links: Literary Connections

Can you link the following literary people or things?

1 The last story in James Joyce's *Dubliners*

The first Mrs Rochester – but in a novel of 1966

Stendhal's 1830 masterpiece (twice over)

The fourth of the *Chronicles of Narnia*

2 (If it helps, this link is sort of linked to the previous link)

Half of Iris Murdoch's only Booker Prize winner

Frank Herbert's bestselling sci-fi series

Virginia Woolf's 1931 stream-of-consciousness novel, tracing a group of friends from childhood to late middle age

Together, the detectives from *Bleak House* and *The Maltese Falcon*

The last two links here are purely factual – between the writers, who you need to identify first from their works.

3 *Not a Penny More, Not a Penny Less*

'To His Coy Mistress'

*The School for Scandal*



 Answers on pp. 165–6

*More than a Game: the Story of Cricket's Early Years*

4 *Kane and Abel*

*Don Quixote*

*The Brothers Karamazov*

*The Pilgrim's Progress*

Answers on pp. 166–7

# Round Five

## Tales from the City: an Urban Round

All the answers here contain or comprise the name of a city – as ever, in a variety of ways.

1 Whose novels include *The Book of Laughter and Forgetting* and *The Unbearable Lightness of Being*?

2 Who wrote the bestselling book about the Kennedy assassination, *The Death of a President*?

3 In the Broadway stories of Damon Runyon, who runs the floating crap game?

4 Which American city is the setting for almost all of the novels of Anne Tyler?

5 Which city is the setting for J. G. Ballard's autobiographical novel, *The Empire of the Sun*?

6 Whose bestselling sort-of-autobiography from 2004 was called *Confessions of an Heiress*?

7 And by way of intellectual contrast, *The Letters of Peter Plymley* was an 1807 defence of Catholic emancipation by which much-quoted literary clergyman?

8 Complete these (also much-quoted) lines from Edgar Allan Poe's 'To Helen': 'To the glory that was Greece . . .'

9 In *The Firm* by John Grisham, in which city is the firm based?





Answers on p. 169

10 With what novel did Ian McEwan win the 1998 Booker Prize?

Answers on p. 169

# Quiz Six: Answers

## Round One

### Devouring Books: Literary Food and Drink

1 John Masefield. The poem is 'Cargoes'.

2 Arnold Wesker

3 It's served in litres and half-litres. Orwell was fiercely opposed to the metric system.

4 Penelope Mortimer, then the wife of John Mortimer

5 Alan Bennett

6 *Three Men in a Boat* by Jerome K. Jerome

7 Laurence Sterne

8 A madeleine cake dipped in tea in Proust's *À la recherche du temps perdu*, which suddenly brought the narrator's memories of his childhood flooding back.

9 Honoré de Balzac. Balzac drank coffee endlessly to fight what he saw as the pointless waste of time represented by sleep. As a result, he wrote the ninety-one novels in his *Comédie humaine* series in just twenty years – and died at fifty-one.

10 Captain Ahab's first mate is Starbuck – after whom the coffee chain is named, because the founders are fans of Melville's novel.

# Round Two

## Dear Sir or Madam: Literature and Letters

1 Oscar Wilde writing to his lover Lord Alfred Douglas (aka 'Bosie') from a family holiday in Babbacombe Cliff, Devon. The letter was later stolen by a blackmailer – and read out in court at Wilde's trials in 1895.

2 Charlotte Brontë writing to a publisher friend about her brother Branwell, and definitely failing to sentimentalise his life in the light of his early death. Branwell, she says in the same letter, was 'his father's and sisters' pride and hope in boyhood – but since manhood, the case has been otherwise'. Both Anne and Emily were younger than their brother, although within nine months both of them were dead too. And just to add to the cheerfulness of this question, Branwell was the model for the violent drunkard in Anne's novel, *The Tenant of Wildfell Hall.* (On a lighter note, as a young man he was once seduced by an older woman called Mrs Robinson.)

3 That was Lord Byron leaving Lady Caroline Lamb in little doubt as to where she stood after an affair that, for all its continuing fame, lasted just five months. Lady Caroline, who famously called Byron 'mad, bad and dangerous to know', put the letter in her novel *Glenarvon*: a not-very-fictional account of their relationship which became a hugely scandalous success in 1816.

A6

The really bad news, though, is that Byron's letter didn't work. Two years after he wrote it, he complained to a friend that Lady Caroline 'comes at all times, at any time, and the moment the door is open, in she walks. She has no shame, no feeling, no one estimable or redeemable quality.'

4 The twenty-six-year-old Henry James writing to his father about George Eliot. In the letter, he did also acknowledge that it was a 'marvel' someone so distinguished should have agreed to his visit at all. (At this stage he'd only published some reviews and short stories in American periodicals.) Nevertheless, in 1878, after another visit, he still seemed to have the same conflict about her appearance. Eliot, he told his brother William, 'has a delightful expression' in 'her large, long, pale equine face'.

5 A characteristically balanced passage from *Stupid White Men* (2001) by Michael Moore – in which the other two questions to George W. Bush are, 'Are you an alcoholic?' and 'Are you a felon?'

6 Ernest Hemingway in nicely relaxed form, writing from Spain to F. Scott Fitzgerald. Good to see there that Hemingway clearly regards drinking wine as not really drinking at all.

## Round Three

### Featured Author: John Keats

1 'A thing of beauty is a joy for ever'

2 Mists – as in 'Season of mists and mellow fruitfulness'

3 Five feet one inch. And that still makes him seven inches taller than the adult Alexander Pope.

4 Woman – from a poem beginning 'Woman! When I behold thee flippant, vain'. According to a witness at the time, when Keats wrote those lines, he 'burst into tears, overpowered by the tenderness of his own imagination'. (To be fair, he was a teenager at the time.)

5 Hampstead – in the garden of Wentworth Place where he was staying with his friend Charles Brown. Wentworth Place is now called Keats House.

6 Fanny Brawne, who lived next door to Wentworth Place

7 'La Belle Dame sans Merci'. (In fact, it contains it twice.)

8 Twenty-five. He died of tuberculosis in Rome in 1821.

9 'Here lies one whose name was writ in water'

10 'Adonais' – parts of which were famously read out by Mick Jagger at a Rolling Stones concert in Hyde Park after Brian Jones had died

# Round Four

## A Round on the Links: Literary Connections



1 SEAS

The last, longest and most acclaimed story in Joyce's *Dubliners* is 'The Dead' – as in, for our purposes, the Dead Sea.

*The Wide Sargasso Sea* is Jean Rhys's (kind of) prequel to *Jane Eyre*, and so concerns the early life in the Caribbean of the girl who ends up as Charlotte Brontë's mad woman in the attic.

Stendhal's 1830 novel is *The Red and the Black* – which are two seas, hence 'twice over'.

The fourth of C. S. Lewis's *The Chronicles of Narnia* is *Prince Caspian* – although, slightly confusingly, it was the second to be published.

2 THINGS YOU'D SEE AT THE SEASIDE

Iris Murdoch won the Booker Prize in 1978 for *The Sea, The Sea*.

Frank Herbert was the author of the multi-million-selling Dune chronicles, beginning with *Dune* itself, the best-selling science-fiction book ever.

Virginia Woolf's *The Waves* is her 1931 novel about that group of friends.

Inspector Bucket is the police inspector in Dickens's

*Bleak House* and Sam Spade is the private eye in Dashiell Hammett's *The Maltese Falcon.*

3 WRITERS WHO WERE ALSO MPS

*Not a Penny More, Not a Penny Less* was the first novel by Jeffrey Archer, elected Conservative MP for the Lincolnshire constituency of Louth in 1969. Five years later, he resigned from parliament when he was declared bankrupt after investing his life savings in a fraudulent Canadian cleaning firm. After that Archer turned to writing as a way – successful, as it turned out – of earning money.

'To His Coy Mistress' (the one that starts 'Had we but world enough and time') is by Andrew Marvell, who was an MP for Hull from 1659 until his death in 1678. Before entering parliament, he'd already been Oliver Cromwell's Latin secretary, a post previously occupied by John Milton. And, should you be wondering, the Latin Secretary was mostly responsible for translating foreign documents.

Richard Brinsley Sheridan wrote the play *The School for Scandal* – as well as *The Rivals* (in which Mrs Malaprop appears). He was MP for Stafford, and had a reputation as a brilliant Commons orator.

*More than a Game* (2007) is by John Major, former MP and indeed PM.

4 WRITERS WHO WENT TO PRISON

*Kane and Abel* was the third novel by Jeffrey Archer, who in 2001 was found guilty of perjury and perverting the course of justice. He served two years of a four-year sentence.

More romantically, Miguel de Cervantes – author of *Don Quixote* – was captured by pirates in 1575 and for the next five years was a prisoner in Algiers. (Later, back in Spain, he was imprisoned at least twice more for financial irregularities.)

In 1849, thirty-one years before publishing *The Brothers Karamazov*, Fyodor Dostoevsky was arrested for being part of a Socialist group, and sent to a Siberian penal settlement for four years. His experiences in the camp were the basis of his book *Notes from the House of the Dead* – and also brought about a religious crisis that turned him from a Socialist into a Christian.



And talking of Christians, from 1660 John Bunyan spent the best part of twelve years in Bedford jail for the serious crime of preaching without a licence. While in prison, Bunyan wrote nine books and started on *The Pilgrim's Progress*, which he continued during another stint in prison in 1675.

## Round Five

### Tales from the City: an Urban Round



1 Milan Kundera

2 William Manchester

3 Nathan Detroit. The stories are the basis of the musical *Guys and Dolls*.

4 Baltimore

5 Shanghai – where Ballard had been a boy during the Japanese invasion

6 Paris Hilton

7 Sydney Smith – Sydney with a 'Y', so he qualifies for this round

8 'And the grandeur that was Rome'

9 Memphis, Tennessee

10 *Amsterdam*

# Quiz Seven

# Round One

## Books and the Arts

1. Which painter's household is the setting for Tracy Chevalier's novel *Girl with a Pearl Earring*?
2. Which bestselling novel of the 1990s centres on a shop called Championship Vinyl?
3. Which literary novelist gave a eulogy at the memorial service for Benny Hill?
4. Which literary novelist wrote the first ever episode of the TV series *Upstairs, Downstairs*?
5. Which playwright played Cyril Kinnear in the film *Get Carter*?
6. Whose novels include *Jazz* and *Song of Solomon*?
7. What's the connection between the crime writer Patricia Cornwell and the painter Walter Sickert?
8. Which Samuel Beckett play shares its title with that of an American sitcom of the 1970s and 80s?
9. Which British winner of the Nobel Prize for Literature used to write for *The Dick Emery Show*?
10. True or false: Kingsley Amis once presented a weekly pop-music show on television?



 Answers on pp. 187–8

# Round Two

## Pedants' Revolt: a Round of Literary Mistakes (II)

So yes, once again, in each of the following passages the author has made some technical or factual error. Can you identify the author, the work – and the mistake in question? (Once again too, if you should happen to be quizzing seriously, there's a point for the book, a point for the author and two for the mistake.)

1 The mistake here only becomes fully clear forty-one chapters later. Nonetheless, it definitely is one – and, given a bit of literary knowledge, can still be spotted from this dramatic passage:

> 'Hold your noise!' cried a terrible voice, as a man started up from among the graves at the side of the church porch. 'Keep still, you little devil, or I'll cut your throat!'
>
> A fearful man, all in coarse grey, with a great iron on his leg. A man with no hat, and with broken shoes, and with an old rag tied round his head. A man who had been soaked in water, and smothered in mud, and lamed by stones, and cut by flints, and stung by nettles, and torn by briars; who limped, and shivered, and glared and growled; and whose teeth chattered in his head as he seized me by the chin.
>
> 'O! Don't cut my throat, sir,' I pleaded in terror. 'Pray don't do it, sir.'





Answers on p. 189

2 (The first name mentioned in this passage is an enormous clue to the 2005 novel from which it comes.)

Arthur believed, in a general way, that God existed, that boys were tempted by sin, and that the Fathers were right to beat them with the Tolley. When it came to particular articles of faith, he argued in private with his friend Partridge. Partridge liked to bamboozle a fellow, and not just on the cricket field.

'Are you aware that the doctrine of the Immaculate Conception became an article of faith as recently as 1854?'

'Somewhat late in the day, I'd have thought, Partridge?'

'Imagine. The Church has been debating the matter for centuries, and all that time it has never been heresy to deny the Virgin Birth. Now it is.'

3 (Quite a tricky mistake this one, so do feel free to guess.)

Then felt I like some watcher of the skies
When a new planet swims into his ken;
Or like stout Cortez when with eagle eyes
He stared at the Pacific – and all his men
Looked at each other with a wild surmise –
Silent, upon a peak in Darien.

4 A phone-call from London to Wall Street in one of the big American novels of the 1980s. (Look out especially for the last name here.)

The plastic speaker was the size of a bedside clock radio. Everyone stared at it, waiting for the voice of

Answers on pp. 189–90 

Gene Lopwitz. Lopwitz was in London where it was now 4.00 pm. He would preside over this meeting by telephone.

'Yeah, I can hear you, Arnie. There was a lotta cheering going on.'

'Where are you, Gene?' asked Arnold Parch.

'I'm at a cricket match.' Then less clearly: 'What's the name a this place again?' He was evidently with some other people. 'Tottenham Park, Arnie. I'm on a kind of terrace.'

'Who's playing?'

'Don't get technical on me, Arnie. A lot of very nice young gentlemen in cable-knit sweaters and white flannel pants, is the best I can tell you.'

Appreciative laughter broke out in the room, and Sherman felt his own lips bending into the somehow obligatory smile.

Q7

Finally in this round, two where the mistakes should be easy enough for especially pedantic ornithologists to spot – but might need a little more guesswork from anybody else.

5 Be innocent of the knowledge, dearest chuck,
Till thou applaud the deed. Come, seeling night,
Scarf up the tender eye of pitiful day,
And with thy bloody and invisible hand
Cancel and tear to pieces that great bond
Which keeps me pale. Light thickens
And the crow makes wing to the rooky wood;
Good things of day begin to droop and drowse,
Whiles night's black agents to their preys do rouse.
Thou marvell'st at my words: but hold thee still.

 Answers on p. 190

Things bad begun make strong themselves by ill.
So, prithee, go with me.

6 This is from a commemorative poem by the poet laureate of the day – which should be the biggest clue. The name of the poem isn't required, so people keeping score should get two points just for that laureate's name.

I'm glad that you are marrying at home
Below Sir Christopher's embracing dome;
Four-square on that his golden cross and ball
Complete our own cathedral of St Paul.
Blackbirds in city churchyards hail the dawn,
Charles and Diana, on your wedding morn.

Answers on p. 191

# Round Three

## Featured Author: Arthur Conan Doyle

1 Where was Doyle a medical student?

2 Which of Doyle's teachers at medical school was, significantly enough, a master of observation, logic, deduction and diagnosis?

3 In the Holmes story 'The Adventure of the Speckled Band', what's the speckled band?

4 What's unusual about the narrator of the Holmes story 'The Adventure of the Blanched Soldier'?

5 Who narrates the story of the Giant Rat of Sumatra?

6 Many of the Holmes stories feature which Scotland Yard inspector?

7 What's the name of Holmes's older and even more brilliant brother?

8 In 'The Adventure of the Final Problem' where does Holmes apparently die?

9 Name any of the three Doyle novels featuring Professor Challenger.

10 For the last ten years of his life, Doyle undertook a worldwide crusade for what?





Answers on pp. 193–4

# Round Four

## A Round on the Links: Literary Connections

Can you link the following literary people or things?

1 John Updike's Harry Angstrom

Mr McGregor's enemy

Roddy Doyle's first three novels (pronunciation-wise)

Richard Adams

2 Dodie Smith's first novel – which still seems to be regarded by fans as her best

The man whose first novel was *Carrie*

The first of the *Canterbury Tales*

The eighteenth-century philosopher George Berkeley

3 Thomas de Quincey

St Augustine

James Hogg

Timothy Lea

4 (Romantically speaking)

Anton Chekhov

Philip Roth

Roald Dahl

Arthur Miller

Q7



Answers on pp. 195–8

# Round Five

## Oh, It's You Again: Literary Characters Who've Been in More than One Book

1. Which historical character features as a baddie in Shakespeare's *Henry VI, Part One* – and has also been the main subject of a burlesque epic by Voltaire, a tragedy by Schiller, a long poem by Robert Southey and dramas by Jean Anouilh and George Bernard Shaw?

2. In the *Harry Potter* novels, what are the four first names of Professor Dumbledore?

3. The 2007 novel *Michael Tolliver Lives* reintroduced the main character from which novel series, published between 1978 and 1990?

4. Who wrote several stories about the Glass family – whose members include Franny and Zooey?

5. Which twelve-novel sequence is narrated by Nicholas Jenkins?

6. Who's the heroine of Emma Tennant's 1993 novel, *Pemberley*?

7. Who created Precious Ramotswe – Botswana's only female private detective?

8. Whose novels *Porno* and *Glue* featured some of the same characters as his first book *Trainspotting*?

9. Name any of the books in Philip Roth's original Zuckerman trilogy.

Q7


Answers on p. 199–200

10 Which long-running fictional character was named after the author of *A Field Guide to the Birds of the West Indies* (1936)?

Answers on p. 200

# Quiz Seven: Answers

## Round One

### Books and the Arts

1. Johannes Vermeer's
2. *High Fidelity* by Nick Hornby. The novel is named after a song by Elvis Costello (not the one of the same name by The Kids from Fame).
3. Anthony Burgess. Burgess believed that Hill's comedy was a masterly study of male sexual regret, and compared him to, among others, Plautus, George Formby, Falstaff, Marie Lloyd and Rabelais.
4. Fay Weldon
5. John Osborne
6. Toni Morrison
7. She thinks Sickert was Jack the Ripper, as explained in her optimistically titled book *Portrait of a Killer: Jack the Ripper – Case Closed.*
8. *Happy Days*. The play featured a woman buried in earth, and the sitcom featured the Fonz.
9. Harold Pinter – strange but true. More middle-aged readers might like to imagine some of Emery's catchphrases delivered in a Pinteresque style: e.g. 'Ooh, you are awful [*menacing pause*] but I like you.'
10. Even stranger but also true. In 1962, he presented eight episodes of *Kingsley Amis Goes Pop* – which

saw Amis perched on a high stool, introducing and interviewing the likes of Billy Fury, Bobby Vee and Rolf Harris. Unforgivably, the tapes were wiped in the late Sixties.

# Round Two

## Pedants' Revolt: a Round of Literary Mistakes (II)

1 That was Pip meeting the convict Magwitch at the beginning of Charles Dickens's *Great Expectations*. But in Chapter Forty-Two, Magwitch reveals that he'd dived off a prison ship and swum to the shore: something that would have been impossible with a Victorian leg-iron on. For a start, he'd never have surfaced after the dive – and even if he had, he couldn't have swum the hundreds of yards from where the ship would have been to the marshes. The simplest explanation for the error, as suggested by John Sutherland in one of his books of literary puzzles, is that Dickens, like most mid-Victorians, just didn't understand swimming – which wouldn't become a popular pastime until later in the century.

2 That was Julian Barnes from *Arthur and George*, in which the Arthur – seen there at Stonyhurst Jesuit School – is Arthur Conan Doyle. But, like many non-Catholics, Barnes has fallen into the trap of thinking that the Immaculate Conception is the same as the Virgin Birth. In fact, it's got nothing to do with the birth or conception of Jesus at all, but is the doctrine that his mother Mary was conceived without original sin. We also know that this was Barnes's mistake rather than Partridge's, because it was corrected for the paperback edition.

3 From 'On First Looking into Chapman's Homer' by

John Keats. Unfortunately, it wasn't Cortez – stout or otherwise – who was silent on a peak in Darien. Keats drew much of the poem's imagery from William Robertson's *The History of America* (1777) and has confused two passages in the book: Cortez's entry into Mexico City, and Balboa's first sighting of the Pacific from the isthmus of Darien.

4 From *The Bonfire of the Vanities*, Tom Wolfe's classic novel of 1980s New York, whose main character, Sherman McCoy, is a Wall Street trader and what was known in those far-off days as a yuppie. Needless to say, however, Tottenham Park is not a London cricket ground of any kind, let alone one big enough to have terracing. It's actually a Jewish cemetery. (By the way, we earlier learned that the meeting is at 10 am New York time, which means that it would be 3, not 4 pm in London.)

5 From Shakespeare's *Macbeth*, with Macbeth dropping dark hints to his wife about the forthcoming murder of Banquo. The Bard's mistake in that passage was pointed out a few years ago in an obsessively ornithological essay by John Crompton in the *Tennyson Research Bulletin*. Crompton started by denouncing Tennyson's bird-based howlers – including having a female nightingale singing – and broadened his attacks from there. Shakespeare's blunder leaves him especially aghast. '*Crows* do not make wing to the *rooky* wood,' he writes sternly. 'The two species do not associate.' His essay ends with the withering question: 'Should A. S. Byatt have won the Booker Prize for *Possession* when she places flocks of ravens in Richmond Park?'

6 From Sir John Betjeman's poem on the royal wedding of July 1981. Sadly, as a Mr K. H. Holdaker immediately explained in a letter to *The Times*, Sir John had mistaken the yearly cycle of the common blackbird. 'I fear not,' wrote Mr Holdaker about the chances of blackbirds hailing that particular dawn. 'It is the moulting season. If you want blackbirds at the wedding, get married in spring.'

# Round Three

## Featured Author: Arthur Conan Doyle

1 Edinburgh University

2 Dr Joseph Bell

3 A snake – to be precise, an Indian swamp adder

4 The narrator is Holmes himself. The only other story he narrates is 'The Adventure of the Lion's Mane'.

5 Nobody. This is one of the adventures we hear about in passing, but which is never told – apparently because, according to Holmes, it's 'a story for which the world is not yet prepared'.

6 Lestrade

7 Mycroft Holmes

8 The Reichenbach Falls in Switzerland. Famously, Doyle killed off Holmes so that he could concentrate on 'more serious literary work'. Even more famously, popular demand forced him to bring back Holmes a few years later. The ledge from which Holmes fell is now marked by a plaque in English, German and French. The English inscription reads: 'At this fearful place, Sherlock Holmes vanquished Professor Moriarty, on 4 May 1891.'

9 *The Poison Belt*, *The Land of Mist* and, best known these days, *The Lost World* – the one about dinosaurs.

10 Spiritualism. His *History of Spiritualism* was published in 1926, and *The Land of Mist* from the same year was a spiritualist novel. At the time, Doyle was by no means the only man of science who saw contacting the dead as the next great scientific challenge. The radio, the telephone and the television were all invented partly because Guglielmo Marconi, Alexander Graham Bell and John Logie Baird believed this too – and thought their inventions might do the trick.

# Round Four

## A Round on the Links: Literary Connections

1 RABBITS (OR IN ONE CASE RABBITTES)

Harry Angstrom is better known as Rabbit in the four Rabbit novels of John Updike. The books, beginning with *Rabbit, Run* (1960), trace Harry's adult life in the Pennsylvanian suburbs from the 1950s to his death in *Rabbit at Rest* (1990).

Peter Rabbit survives a hair-raising chase after raiding Mr McGregor's vegetables in *The Tale of Peter Rabbit* by Beatrix Potter. (Before the action of the book begins, Mr McGregor has already killed Peter's father and put him in a pie.)

The Rabbitte family star in all of Roddy Doyle's first three novels: *The Commitments*, *The Snapper* and *The Van* – now collectively called *The Barrytown Trilogy*.

Richard Adams's first novel was the firmly rabbit-based *Watership Down*, rejected by at least twelve publishers before it became a worldwide bestseller and a hit film that provided a number one single for Art Garfunkel.

2 CHESS PIECES

Thanks to Disney, Dodie Smith may be most famous for *The Hundred and One Dalmatians* –

but in the 1930s she'd been a successful playwright, before turning to fiction with *I Capture the Castle*, published when she was fifty-two. The book sold over a million copies, and its celebrity champions since have included Ralph Vaughan Williams, Joanna Trollope and J. K. Rowling.

Stephen King began his multi-million selling career in 1974 with *Carrie*, written in the laundry room of the rented trailer he, his wife and their two children were living in at the time. King went on to become second only to Shakespeare as the author whose work has been most often turned into films.

The first of Chaucer's *Canterbury Tales*, after the General Prologue, is 'The Knight's Tale'.

George Berkeley is more usually known as Bishop Berkeley, largely because he was the Bishop of Cloynes. Berkeley's idea that things exist only in that they are perceived led to the question: 'If a tree falls in a forest and nobody is there to hear it, does it make a sound?' It also inspired a limerick by Monsignor Ronald Knox:

> There was once a man who said, 'God
> Must think it exceedingly odd
>   If he finds that this tree
>   Continues to be
> When there's no one about in the Quad.'

This in turn inspired the anonymous reply:

> Dear Sir, Your astonishment's odd:
> *I* am always about in the Quad.
>   And that's why the tree

Will continue to be,
Since observed by Yours faithfully, God.

3 CONFESSIONS

Thomas de Quincey made his name in 1822 with *Confessions of an English Opium Eater* – written when opium was as easily obtainable, and as legal, as aspirin is today. The book did much to draw attention to its dangers.

St Augustine's *Confessions* is often described as the first autobiography, as well as being the only fourth-century work of theology to appear in this book. It contains the popular prayer: 'Oh, Master, make me chaste and celibate – but not yet!' (The Penguin Classics edition was translated by a man called R. S. Pine-Coffin.)

James Hogg was already known as a poet when, in 1824, he published his only novel, *The Private Memoirs and Confessions of a Justified Sinner*, now considered a Calvinist classic.



Last and – let's face it – least, Timothy Lea wrote all those 1970s sex-comedy novels like *Confessions of a Driving Instructor* and *Confessions of a Window Cleaner*, many of which became films starring Robin Askwith as Timothy Lea and Cherie Blair's dad, Tony Booth, as Sidney Noggett.

4 THEY ALL MARRIED ACTRESSES

Chekhov used to say that a man should never marry an actress – until he did. She was Olga Knipper of the Moscow Art Theatre, who played Masha in the first production of *Three Sisters*, and Ranyevskaya in that of *The Cherry Orchard*. She played Ranyevskaya again in 1945 as part of the Soviet celebrations for the victory over Hitler – by which time Chekhov had been dead for forty-one years.

Funnily enough, Claire Bloom was also playing Ranyevskaya in *The Cherry Orchard* when her marriage to Philip Roth reached its grisly crisis point. According to her autobiography, *Leaving a Doll's House*, Roth's demands in the divorce settlement included $150 an hour for the time they'd spent discussing her scripts. He also wanted $62 billion for her failure to honour their prenuptial agreement.

Roald Dahl's first wife was the American actress Patricia Neal, who co-starred in *Breakfast at Tiffany's* and won a Best Actress Oscar in 1963 for *Hud*.

Arthur Miller and Marilyn Monroe you probably know about – but his autobiography *Timebends* contains a particularly vivid description of the effect her beauty had on him when they first met. 'The sight of her was something like pain,' writes Miller, 'and I knew I must flee or walk into a doom beyond all knowing.' Understandably, he opted for the doom.

## Round Five

### Oh, It's You Again: Literary Characters Who've Been in More than One Book

1 Joan of Arc

2 Albus Percival Wulfric Brian

3 The *Tales of the City* series by Armistead Maupin

4 J. D. Salinger. 'Franny' and 'Zooey' were also the titles of two of the stories.

5 *A Dance to the Music of Time* by Anthony Powell

6 Elizabeth Bennet. *Pemberley* is Tennant's sequel to *Pride and Prejudice*, taking its title from the name of Mr Darcy's house in the original book. The sequel picked up the story a year after Elizabeth had married Mr Darcy, and suggested the marriage wasn't going well. Tennant also wrote *Emma in Love* – in which Austen's heroine found some consolation for her unconsummated marriage to Mr Knightley by having a lesbian affair. These novels have not, on the whole, gone down well with Austen fans.

7 Alexander McCall Smith

8 Irvine Welsh's

9 *The Ghost Writer*, *Zuckerman Unbound* and *The Anatomy Lesson* – although Nathan Zuckerman went on to appear in several more Roth novels after that. Picking up from the last round, one of them is *I Married a Communist*, about a man who's traduced

in the autobiography of his ex-wife, a wildly self-dramatising actress.

10 James Bond. Ian Fleming, a keen bird-watcher, had a copy of the book in his house in Jamaica – and took the name of its author, he later explained, because 'I wanted the simplest, dullest, plainest-sounding name I could find. "James Bond" was much better than something more interesting, like "Peregrine Carruthers".' In the film *Die Another Day* Pierce Brosnan as Bond is seen reading *A Field Guide to the Birds of the West Indies* when he's in Cuba posing as an ornithologist.

Picking up from the last round too, Timothy Lea was a pseudonym for Christopher Wood who, under his real name, wrote the screenplays for two Bond films, including *Moonraker* – which ends in best Timothy Lea style. Bond is in a space shuttle with Holly Goodhead, and 'Q' says, 'I think he's attempting re-entry.'

# Quiz Eight

# Round One

## A Literary Flowering: Books and Botany

1. Which 1951 novel describes murderous plants taking over the world?
2. Which British Nobel Prize-winner's first novel was *The Grass is Singing*?
3. Whose first collection of poetry was *Leaves of Grass*?
4. Who wrote *The Camomile Lawn*?
5. Which floral first name is shared by the authors of *Music and Silence* and *The Towers of Trebizond*?
6. Who wrote the children's classic *The Secret Garden*?
7. In Kenneth Grahame's *The Wind in the Willows*, the Mole and the Rat have a mystical vision of which god?
8. Which twentieth-century poem begins with these lines?

   April is the cruellest month, breeding
   Lilacs out of the dead land.

9. What event of July 1986 was the subject of the poem 'The Honey Bee and the Thistle' by Ted Hughes, the poet laureate at the time?
10. Whose last novel was *The Blue Flower*?





Answers on p. 219

# Round Two

## Literary Feuds and Rivalries

Six extracts on a subject that's been around since at least the time Aristophanes first attacked Euripides in several plays of the fifth century BC . . .

1 From the diary of a writer sometimes thought of as a bit of a snob – which given this entry doesn't seem entirely unfair. Who's the writer and who, for a giveaway point, is she writing about?

16 August 1922

I should be reading *Ulysses*, and fabricating my case for and against. I have read 200 pages so far – not a third; and have been amused, stimulated, charmed, interested, by the first 2 or 3 chapters; and then puzzled, bored, irritated and disillusioned by a queasy undergraduate scratching his pimples. An illiterate, underbred book it seems to me; the book of a self taught working man, and we all know how distressing they are, how egotistic, insistent; raw, striking; and ultimately nauseating.

Q8

2 From a 1991 volume of memoirs, complete with geographical clue. Again, writer and victim please . . .

While I was in Wales, I encountered the poet in the flesh. Apart from just one poem, 'The Hunchback in the Park', which distinguishes itself from all the rest of his poetic output by not being about him, and a few



Answers on p. 221

isolated lines from other poems – 'And death shall have no dominion', 'Deep with the first dead lies London's daughter' – he strikes me as a very bad poet indeed, or else a brilliant one in a mode that is anathema to me. Either way he is a pernicious figure, one who has helped to get Wales and Welsh poetry a bad name and generally done lasting harm to both. The general picture he draws of the place and the people is false, sentimentalising, melodramatising, sensationalising, ingratiating.

3 A self-deprecating piece of rivalry now, from a surprise non-fiction bestseller of 2004. You need to identify the book and author this time – and the bits before and after the rivalry part might help. The scene is the Toronto literary festival, where that author has just been interviewed and is about to await his public for a book-signing.

I smoked a cigarette in a marked-off smoking cubicle, was led to a chair in the lobby, where a quarter of a dozen people waited with books for me to sign – one of them by the biographer Michael Holroyd, the rest by me. At a table a few yards from mine the novelist David Lodge, who had been simultaneously interviewed in an adjacent theatre, was faced with a queue that seemed to stretch right out of the lobby on to the pavement, and beyond that possibly all the way to the airport, where planes containing David Lodge fans were even now stacking in the air.

I had the advantage of him, though, in being able to get away within minutes, and within a few more minutes Victoria and I were in the hotel. The lobby's

Answers on p. 221

only distinguishing feature is that you can't smoke in it, nor can you smoke in any of the several public rooms, nor at the very long bar that stretches across half the lobby, and at which nobody was drinking when we went by – in fact, nothing about it suggested that authentic bar life flowed and ebbed there – affairs started, marriages ended, births drunk to, dead friends toasted.

4 Who's this defending himself with some vigour – after being attacked by a celebrated contemporary for his 'politically Conservative' school stories?

The basic political assumptions of my books, Mr Orwell goes on, are two: that nothing ever changes, and that foreigners are funny. Well, the French have a proverb that the more a thing changes, the more it is just the same. As for foreigners being funny, I must shock Mr Orwell by telling him that foreigners *are* funny. They lack the sense of humour which is the special gift to our own chosen nation: and people without a sense of humour are always unconsciously funny. Take Hitler, for example; in England the play-acting ass would be laughed out of existence. Take Mussolini – can anyone imagine a fat man in London talking the balderdash that Benito talks in Rome to wildly-cheering audiences, without evoking, not wild cheers, but inextinguishable laughter.




Answers on p. 222

Helpful note: the last two writers in this round have both been featured authors earlier in the book.

5 Who wrote this 1997 letter to the *Guardian*?

Anyone reading yesterday's letters from Salman Rushdie and Christopher Hitchens might well ask himself into whose hands the great cause of free speech has fallen. Whether from Rushdie's throne or Hitchens' gutter, the message is the same: 'Our cause is absolute, it brooks no dissent; whoever questions it is by definition an ignorant, pompous, semi-literate unperson.'

Two rabid Ayatollahs could not have done a better job. But will the friendship last? I am amazed that Hitchens has put up with Rushdie's self-canonisation for so long.

Rushdie, so far as I can make out, does not deny that he has insulted a great religion. Instead he accuses me of taking the Philistine reductionist radical Islamist line. I didn't know I was so clever. What I do know is, Rushdie took on a known enemy and screamed 'foul' when it acted in character.

6 Another long-standing feud becomes the basis of a short story, where the first speaker here is telling the narrator about the alarming behaviour of his brother-in-law. Who wrote the story – and who, fairly obviously, is the model for the brother-in-law?

'Do you know where Rodney is at this moment? Up in the nursery, bending over his son Timothy's cot, gathering material for a poem about the unfortunate little rat when asleep. Some baloney, no doubt, about

Answers on pp. 222–3

how he hugs his teddy bear and dreams of angels. Yes, that is what he is doing, writing poetry about Timothy. Horrible whimsical stuff that . . . Well, when I tell you that he refers to him throughout as "Timothy Bobbin", you will appreciate what we are up against.'

I am not a weak man, but I confess that I shuddered.

'Timothy Bobbin?'

'Timothy by golly Bobbin. No less.'

Q8


Answers on p. 222–3

## Round Three

### Featured Author: William Shakespeare

1 If Shakespeare's plays were arranged in alphabetical order by title, which one would come first?

2 What connects Shakespeare's mother with the setting of *As You Like It*?

3 Which stage direction explains the disappearance of Antigonus from *The Winter's Tale*?

4 What's the only Shakespeare play whose title contains an English place-name?

5 Which Shakespearean main character speaks the line: 'Why, there they are both, baked in this pie'?

6 In *Romeo and Juliet*, is Romeo a Montague or a Capulet?

7 Between 1788 and 1820 why was *King Lear* not allowed to be performed in Britain?

8 What's the only Premier League football club named after a Shakespearean character?

9 In *Othello*, who kills Iago?

10 To the nearest thousand, how many direct descendants of Shakespeare are thought to be alive today?



 Answers on p. 225

## Round Four

### A Round on the Links: Literary Connections

Can you link the following literary people or things? (And this time, in honour of the featured author, the round is something of a Shakespeare special.)

1 Michel Faber's big 2002 bestseller about a Victorian prostitute

The best-known literary creation by Baroness Orczy

Jeanette Winterson's third novel, whose title *proves* that oranges are not the only fruit

Cordelia's unsuccessful suitor in *King Lear*

2 *White Fang*

The 1998 play by Michael Frayn featuring Niels Bohr and Werner Heisenberg talking quantum physics

The twentieth-century philosopher whose 1978 essay collection *Russian Thinkers* included the highly influential 'The Hedgehog and the Fox'?

Juliet's unsuccessful suitor in *Romeo and Juliet*

(Clue: Rigsby's cat in *Rising Damp* would be in the same category)

3 Montmorency the Dog

Luigi Pirandello

Q8



Answers on pp. 227–8

Lord Peter Wimsey's tailors

The Shakespeare play that's subtitled *What You Will*

4 The Woolfs' publishing firm

The fourth novel by the man whose first was *Digital Fortress*

Elbow in *Measure for Measure* . . .

. . . and the man whom Mark Twain believed wrote *Measure for Measure*

Answers on pp. 228–9

# Round Five

## Simply Seek Similar Sounds: an Alliterative Round

All the answers here are literary people or things with alliterative names – and, in the usual helpful way of this book, over the course of the round the alliteration comes in alphabetical order.

1 In which 1968 novel by J. P. Donleavy is the main character in love with Miss Fitzdare?

2 Who, for every one of the seventeen years until 2003, was the most borrowed author from British libraries?

3 What was the last novel by George Eliot?

4 Which German author won the 1999 Nobel Prize for Literature?

5 Which German-Swiss author, later a favourite of the hippies of the 1960s, wrote *Siddhartha* and *The Glass Bead Game*?

6 Who's the only alliterative eponymous main character in a novel by Charles Dickens?

7 What's the only poem now attributed to Chaucer's contemporary William Langland?

8 Which crime novelist has also written under the name Barbara Vine?

9 Which war poet also wrote an autobiographical

Q8



Answers on p. 231

trilogy of novels, published together in 1937 as *The Complete Memoirs of George Shearston*?

10 Who's the most famous literary creation of the Reverend Wilbert Awdry?

Answers on p. 231

# Quiz Eight: Answers

# Round One

## A Literary Flowering: Books and Botany

1. *The Day of the Triffids* by John Wyndham
2. Doris Lessing
3. Walt Whitman
4. Mary Wesley
5. Rose – the authors being Rose Tremain and Rose Macaulay respectively
6. Frances Hodgson Burnett, who also wrote *Little Lord Fauntleroy*
7. Pan – in the chapter 'The Piper at the Gates of Dawn', which also gave Pink Floyd the title of their first album
8. *The Waste Land* by T. S. Eliot
9. The marriage of Prince Andrew and Sarah Ferguson. (The poem contains the lines, spoken by Prince Andrew, 'A helicopter snatched you up./ The pilot it was me.' )
10. Penelope Fitzgerald

# Round Two

## Literary Feuds and Rivalries

1 Virginia Woolf ponders James Joyce and his recently published novel, *Ulysses* – although it was so rude that it couldn't be published anywhere but Paris. All these years later, Woolf is surely still the only reader of *Ulysses* to have found the book 'illiterate'.

2 Kingsley Amis giving Dylan Thomas a thorough kicking in the chapter from his *Memoirs* on his time in Swansea. The kicking goes on for several pages, before Amis delivers the concise summary: 'Dylan Thomas was an outstandingly unpleasant man, one who cheated and stole from his friends and peed on their carpets.' It was also while he was in Swansea, lecturing in English at the university, that Amis published *Lucky Jim*. By the time of those *Memoirs* in 1991, the city had 'again become what it was further back in my life: the piece of earth I know best, better than any part of London, and feel most at home in'.

3 By no means the only passage from Simon Gray's *The Smoking Diaries* where the sixty-a-day playwright lamented the plight of the modern smoker. (These days, of course, he'd have been lucky to get a marked-off cubicle.) Mathematically minded readers will also have spotted that 'a quarter of a dozen' people with books for him to sign means three – including the person with the Michael Holroyd.

A8

4 Those were 129 of the approximately 75 million published words written by Frank Richards, the author of the Billy Bunter books and much else besides – and a man who for decades averaged more than ten thousand words a day. Indeed, he was so prolific that in 'Boys' Weeklies', the essay in *Horizon* magazine which inspired that reply, George Orwell had presumed that 'Frank Richards' must be the pseudonym for an entire writing team. (Actually it was the pseudonym for one bloke called Charles Hamilton.) As a result, Orwell was amazed when the letter arrived. It was printed in *Horizon* in 1940 to the delight of the literary world.

5 John le Carré having one of his many pops at Salman Rushdie in their long-standing feud over the *Satanic Verses* affair. Rushdie naturally didn't take any of the attacks lying down.

6 That was P. G. Wodehouse in a story called 'Rodney Has a Relapse' – where the poet Rodney Spelvin becomes a chance for Wodehouse to have a vigorous swipe at A. A. Milne. Presumably, Wodehouse was being so uncharacteristically vicious because in 1941, when he made his controversial broadcasts from Germany (as mentioned in Quiz Two), Milne had been one of his severest critics. And just to make sure we don't miss the point, Wodehouse also gives us some of Spelvin's Timothy Bobbin poems – one of which goes like this:

> Timothy Bobbin has ten little toes.
> He takes them out walking wherever he goes.

And if Timothy gets a cold in the head,
His ten little toes stay with him in bed.

In the story, the brother-in-law also goes on to say that Rodney 'is laying up a lifetime of shame and misery for the wretched little moppet' – which is certainly what happened in Christopher Robin's case. The adult Christopher Milne once described his dad's poem 'Vespers' (the one about Christopher Robin saying his prayers) as 'a toe-curling, fist-clenching, lip-biting' source of embarrassment.

A8

# Round Three

## Featured Author: William Shakespeare

1 *All's Well that Ends Well*

2 The word 'Arden'. Shakespeare's mother's maiden name was Mary Arden, and the setting of *As You Like It* is the Forest of Arden.

3 'Exit, pursued by a bear'

4 *The Merry Wives of Windsor*

5 Titus Andronicus – explaining to Tamora the whereabouts of her two sons, whom he's slaughtered and put in the pie she's just been eating

6 A Montague

7 Because it portrayed a fictional mad king at a time when Britain had a real mad king in George III

8 Tottenham Hotspur – as in Harry Hotspur, real name Henry Percy, from *Henry IV Part One*. Percy's descendants owned land on Tottenham Marshes and his dashing character appealed to the founders of the club.

9 A slight trick question, this one. The answer is nobody. Iago is still alive at the end of the play, although he is about to be dragged off and tortured.

10 Another slight trick question. The answer is none – his last grandchild, Elizabeth Hall, died childless in 1670.

# Round Four

## A Round on the Links: Literary Connections

1 SHADES OF RED

Michel Faber's nine-hundred-page bestseller was *The Crimson Petal and the White.*

Baroness Orczy created the Scarlet Pimpernel – definitely better known than her later creation, the aristocratic female detective, Lady Molly of Scotland Yard.

Jeanette Winterson's third novel was *Sexing the Cherry* in 1989. (And just in case you were mystified by the phrasing, her first was *Oranges Are Not the Only Fruit.*) Five years later, one critic said of Winterson that 'no one working in the English language comes close to matching' Winterson's 'exuberance, passion and fidelity to words'. The name of the critic was Jeanette Winterson.

A8

The Duke of Burgundy asks for Cordelia's hand in the first scene of Shakespeare's *King Lear* – but loses out to the King of France, mainly because he won't take her without a dowry.

2 CAPITAL CITIES

*White Fang*, the 1906 tale of a dog in the Klondike gold rush, is by Jack London.

The Michael Frayn play is Copenhagen – based on Bohr and Heisenberg's meeting there in 1941.

*Russian Thinkers* was by Isaiah Berlin. In the programme for the New York production of his trilogy *The Coast of Utopia* in 2006, Tom Stoppard mentioned how much Berlin's book had influenced the plays – which, much to the publishers' surprise, led to it suddenly being in hot demand.

Count Paris is Juliet's suitor and the man her parents want her to marry in Shakespeare's play – before she falls for Romeo instead.

(Oh yes, and Rigsby's cat is called Vienna.)

### 3 THE THREE TIMES TABLE

Montmorency is from *Three Men in a Boat* by Jerome K. Jerome, and even makes it into the subtitle: *To Say Nothing of the Dog!*

Pirandello was the Italian avant-garde author and dramatist who won the Nobel Prize for Literature in 1934 – and whose most performed play is *Six Characters in Search of an Author*.

*The Nine Tailors* is one of the Lord Peter Wimsey novels by Dorothy L. Sayers, with the title referring to a pattern of bell-ringing.

*What You Will* is the subtitle of *Twelfth Night*.

### 4 THE NAMES OF ARTISTS

Virginia Woolf and husband Leonard founded the Hogarth Press. This was named after Hogarth

House where they were living at the time, and became an early publisher of T. S. Eliot, along with translations of Tolstoy and Chekhov.

*Digital Fortress* was the first novel by Dan Brown – and his fourth was *The Da Vinci Code*, so successful that *Digital Fortress* and his other books were soon reissued and became bestsellers too.

Elbow in *Measure for Measure* is a constable – for our purposes, as in John.

In his book *Is Shakespeare Dead?* Mark Twain was another of the distinguished men of his day to go along with the theory that Shakespeare's plays were written by Francis Bacon – also the name of a twentieth-century British painter. To be scrupulously accurate, what Twain said was: 'I only *believed* Bacon wrote Shakespeare, whereas I *knew* Shakespeare didn't.'

## Round Five

### Simply Seek Similar Sounds: an Alliterative Round

1. *The Beastly Beatitudes of Balthasar B* – which clearly had to feature in this round somewhere. Donleavy's other books include *The Saddest Summer of Samuel S*, *The Destinies of Darcy Dancer, Gentleman* – and, on a less alliterative note, *A Fairy Tale of New York*, which gave the Pogues the title of their most famous song.
2. Catherine Cookson, whose reign was eventually ended by Jacqueline Wilson. (In 1988, a third of all the books borrowed from British libraries were by Cookson.)
3. *Daniel Deronda*
4. Gunter Grass – perhaps most famous in this country for *The Tin Drum* and, these days, for his possible Nazi past
5. Herman Hesse – also a Nobel Prize-winner in 1946
6. Nicholas Nickleby
7. *Piers Plowman* – which, suitably for this round, was a product of the medieval Alliterative Revival
8. Ruth Rendell
9. Siegfried Sassoon. The novels were *Memoirs of a Fox-Hunting Man*, *Memoirs of an Infantry Officer* and *Shearston's Progress*.
10. *Thomas the Tank Engine*

# Quiz Nine

## Round One

### The Five Senses

1 Who created the famously deaf Quasimodo, the hunchback of Notre-Dame?

2 Who created the famously smelly Fungus the Bogeyman?

3 Who wrote the 1985 novel *Perfume*?

4 *Touching the Void* was a non-fiction bestseller by whom?

5 Which then-teenager wrote the play *A Taste of Honey*?

6 Charles Warrell created which series of popular children's books – encouraging children to spot the things around them?

7 Which E. M. Forster novel contains a celebrated tribute to Beethoven's Fifth Symphony?

8 Who won the American National Book Award in 1985 with *White Noise*?

9 In which novel would you find blind Pew?

10 Who wrote this two-line poem?

> Men seldom make passes
> At girls who wear glasses.





Answers on p. 247

# Round Two

## What Happened Next?

This round features extracts that immediately precede lines of prose or poetry that are now very famous indeed. Your challenge, as you might imagine, is to identify what entry in every dictionary of quotations ever since is about to come next. (In the case of the poetry, of course, the rhyme scheme should help.) Double points if you can do this just from the extract itself. Normal points if you need the name of the author and work first – and these can all be found at the back of the book on p. 286.

1 In the Spring a fuller crimson comes upon the robin's breast;
In the Spring the wanton lapwing gets himself another crest;
In the Spring a livelier iris changes on the burnish'd dove . . .

Q9

2 Anything approaching the change that came over his features I have never seen before, and hope never to see again. Oh, I wasn't touched. I was fascinated. It was as though a veil had been rent. I saw on that ivory face the expression of sombre pride, of ruthless power, of craven terror – of an intense and hopeless despair. Did he live his life again in every detail of desire, temptation, and surrender during that supreme moment of complete knowledge? He cried


Answers on p. 249

in a whisper at some image, at some vision – he cried out twice, a cry that was no more than a breath . . .

3 No Place so Sacred from such Fops is barr'd,
Nor is Paul's Church more safe than Paul's Church-
yard:
Nay, fly to Altars; there they'll talk you dead;
For . . .

4 No man is an island, entire of itself; every man is a piece of the continent, a part of the main. If a clod be washed away by the sea, Europe is the less, as well as if a promontory were; any man's death diminishes me, because I am involved in mankind; and therefore never send to know . . .

5 If you can dream – and not make dreams your
master
If you can think – and not make thoughts your
aim . . .

6 (A slightly trickier rhyme scheme here, but it still should help)

The year's at the spring
And day's at the morn;
Morning's at seven;
The hillside's dew-pearled;
The lark's on the wing;
The snail's on the thorn:

Answers on pp. 249–50

# Round Three

## Featured Author: Agatha Christie

1 What's the name of Miss Marple's village?

2 What kind of novels did Christie publish under the pseudonym of Mary Westmacott?

3 In what context did Christie use the pseudonym of Teresa Neele?

4 *The Mousetrap* opened in London in 1952. Within three years either way, in which year did it become the longest-running play in British theatrical history?

5 Who connects the first London production of *The Mousetrap* with Gandhi and Steve Biko?

6 What's the British title of the book published in America as *What Mrs McGillicuddy Saw*?

7 What was the profession of Christie's second husband, Max Mallowan?

8 Who once called Hercule Poirot 'a detestable, bombastic, tiresome, egocentric little creep'?

9 Where did Christie get the title for her 1962 novel *The Mirror Crack'd from Side to Side*?

10 What was Hercule Poirot's last case?





Answers on pp. 251–2

# Round Four

## A Round on the Links: Literary Connections

Can you link the following literary people or things?

1 Joanne Harris

Arthur Dent

The origin of men, according to John Gray

A dramatic success for J. M. Barrie in 1901

2 (These come in the right order)

Laurie Lee's 1969 follow-up to *Cider with Rosie*

Arthur Koestler's 1940 attack on Stalinism

Ernest Hemingway's 1932 celebration of bullfighting

Mark Haddon's bestselling novel, narrated by an autistic child

A couple more of the purely factual ones now. This time, the link in each case is between four novels – although you do sometimes have to work out what those novels are . . .

Q9

3 Jay McInerney's *Bright Lights, Big City*

Graham Greene's novel about a priest on the run in the Mexican revolution

Henry James's *The Turn of the Screw*

Sinister goings-on at Manderley

 Answers on pp. 253–5

4 The 1847 novel narrated by Lockwood and Nelly Dean

*The Bell Jar*

Scarlett O'Hara living in Tara

*Savrola* by Winston Churchill

Answers on pp. 255–6

# Round Five

## Body of Literature: a Biological Round

All the answers here contain or comprise a part of the human body.

1. Which novel of 2000 begins with Archie Jones attempting suicide on Cricklewood Broadway?
2. In which bestseller of 1974 are the main (human) characters Martin Brody, Matt Hooper and Quint?
3. What's the first phrase of Virgil's *Aeneid*? (In English will do.)
4. What's the first word – and indeed, the second, third, fourth and fifth word – of Tom Stoppard's *Rosencrantz and Guildenstern Are Dead*?
5. What's the title of Christy Brown's autobiography?
6. What was Alice Sebold's bestselling debut novel?
7. Which 1970 book by Dee Brown did much to make the American public aware of the fate of Native Americans in the nineteenth century? (Clue: the title contains two body parts.)
8. Whose novels of the 1990s included *Aunt Margaret's Lover*, *Sleeping Beauties* and *Janice Gentle Gets Sexy*?
9. Sue Trinder is the main character in which Sarah Waters novel?



 Answers on p. 257

10 What's the title of John Lahr's biography of Joe Orton, which later became a successful film?

Answers on p. 257

# Quiz Nine: Answers

## Round One

### The Five Senses

1 Victor Hugo – in *Notre-Dame de Paris*

2 Raymond Briggs

3 Patrick Süskind

4 Joe Simpson

5 Shelagh Delaney

6 The *I-Spy* books. (Back in those less enlightened times, Warrell was known as Big Chief I-Spy.)

7 *Howards End*, where Forster calls the symphony 'the most sublime noise that has ever penetrated into the ear of man'.

8 Don DeLillo

9 *Treasure Island* by Robert Louis Stevenson

10 Dorothy Parker. The poem is called 'News Item'.

# Round Two

## What Happened Next?

1 'In the Spring a young man's fancy lightly turns to thoughts of love.'

There's a nice (and surely accurate) parody of Tennyson's sentiments by E. Y. Harburg, the man who wrote 'Over the Rainbow':

> In the Spring a young man's fancy lightly turns
> to thoughts of love;
> And in summer,
> And in autumn,
> And in winter –
> See above.

2 'The horror! The horror!' The dying words of Mr Kurtz, which possibly became even more famous when spoken by Marlon Brando in *Apocalypse Now*, a film that updated Conrad's story to the Vietnam War.

A9

3 'Fools rush in where Angels fear to tread' – one of the few lines of eighteenth-century poetry to feature in songs by both Frank Sinatra and Elvis Presley, as well as the title of an E. M. Forster novel. Nor it is the only phrase from 'An Essay on Criticism' that's entered the language. The poem also contains: 'To err is human, to forgive, divine', 'A little learning is a dangerous thing', and 'What oft was thought but

ne'er so well expressed'. Pope was twenty-one when he wrote it.

4 '. . . for whom the bells tolls; it tolls for thee.'

5 'If you can meet with Triumph and Disaster
And treat those two impostors just the same'

6 'God's in His heaven –
All's right with the world!'

On a less lovely note, 'Pippa Passes' has also become notorious for containing the word 'twats' – which, though Browning didn't realise it, has always had the same meaning as it does today. The story goes that when the editors of the *Oxford English Dictionary* wrote to ask what he meant by it, Browning replied that it was a piece of headgear for nuns. He knew this because he'd once read a poem called 'Vanity of Vanities' published in 1659, which attacked an over-ambitious priest with the lines:

> They talk't of his having a Cardinall's Hat;
> They'd send him as soon an Old Nun's Twat.

## Round Three

### Featured Author: Agatha Christie

1 St Mary Mead

2 Romances. The fact that Christie and Westmacott were one and the same remained a secret for the first four of the six Westmacott novels – until the *Sunday Times* revealed all in 1949.

3 During her mysterious disappearance in 1926, when she apparently suffered a nervous breakdown. The discovery of her abandoned car led to intense media speculation and national appeals for information. Christie was eventually found nearly two weeks later in a Harrogate hotel under the name Mrs Teresa Neele – which also seems to have been the name of her then husband's mistress. Perhaps not surprisingly, the incident went unmentioned in her autobiography.

4 1958 – and forty-four years later it was still going strong enough for the Queen to attend the fiftieth anniversary Royal Gala Performance. (In Canada, mind you, the play did less well: opening in 1977 and closing after just twenty-six and a half years.) Back in 1952, Christie had signed over any royalties the play might earn to her seven-year-old grandson as a little gift.

5 Richard Attenborough – who was in the original cast and went on to direct films about Gandhi (*Gandhi*) and Biko (*Cry Freedom*)

6 *4.50 from Paddington* – in which Mrs McGillicuddy, an old friend of Miss Marple's, sees a murder on a passing train

7 He was an archaeologist, specialising in Iraq and Syria.

8 Agatha Christie – in 1960 during one of her many periods of being a bit sick of her best-loved creation. As early as 1938 she'd made the slightly gentler point, 'There are moments when I have felt: "Why – why – why did I ever invent this detestable, bombastic, tiresome little man?"'

9 From Tennyson's 'The Lady of Shalott'. ('The mirror crack'd from side to side;/ "The curse is come upon me," cried/ The Lady of Shalott.') The book was dedicated to Margaret Rutherford, the first actress to play Miss Marple in a film.

10 *Curtain* – a book written in the 1940s, and originally intended to be published posthumously. In the event, it came out in 1975, the year before Christie's death, when she realised she could no longer write novels. Poirot dies in the book and, following its publication, he became the only fictional character to receive an obituary in the *New York Times*.

# Round Four

## A Round on the Links: Literary Connections

1 CHOCOLATE

Joanne Harris hit the literary big time in 1999 with her novel *Chocolat*.

Arthur Dent is the main character in *The Hitch Hiker's Guide to the Galaxy* series by Douglas Adams.

John Gray's *Men Are from Mars, Women Are from Venus* was one of the biggest sellers of the 1990s – and a big favourite of Bridget Jones's. Other women have been less enthusiastic. One female critic, for example, has described the book as 'a sexist, patronizing, male-centered invective which does little more than perpetuate long-held negative gender stereotypes'.

J. M. Barrie's 1901 success was with his play *Quality Street* – three years before he had an even bigger one with *Peter Pan*. And *Quality Street* must still have been pretty well known in 1936, because that's when Nestlé launched a new collection of chocolates and decided to name it after the play. For many years, the two figures on the box were Barrie's two principal characters, Phoebe Throssel and Valentine Brown.

Lee's *As I Walked out One Midsummer Morning*, the second volume of his autobiography, takes him from Gloucestershire via London and on to Spain, then on the eve of civil war.

Koestler had himself been a Communist, but left the party in 1938 because of Stalin's show trials, which form the basis of his novel *Darkness at Noon*. Koestler's later interests included LSD, Eastern religion and euthanasia. In 1983, suffering from Parkinson's disease and leukaemia, he committed suicide, along with his wife, leaving a will that endowed a chair of parapsychology at the University of Edinburgh. Among his fans is Sting, who named the Police album *The Ghost in the Machine* after a Koestler book.

Actually, 'celebration' may be too small a word for Hemingway's attitude to bullfighting in *Death in the Afternoon*. He saw it as, among other things, a ballet, a test of essential manhood and proof of 'the emotional and spiritual intensity and pure classic beauty that can be produced by a man, an animal, and a piece of scarlet serge draped on a stick'.

Mark Haddon's bestseller was 2003's *The Curious Incident of the Dog in the Night-Time*, a title taken from a line in the Sherlock Holmes story 'The Adventure of the Silver Blaze'. Because Christopher, the fifteen-year-old narrator, is fascinated by prime numbers, the novel begins with Chapter Two, and ends fifty-one chapters later with Chapter Two Hundred and Thirty-three.

3 NOVELS WITH UNNAMED MAIN CHARACTERS

*Bright Lights, Big City* is written in the second person – as in 'You are at a nightclub talking to a girl with a shaved head' – so we never learn the name of the party-going, coke-snorting protagonist in 1980s Manhattan. Nor do we ever find out the name of the whisky priest in Greene's *The Power and the Glory*. Nor of the governess who narrates the ghostly goings-on with her charges Miles and Flora in *The Turn of the Screw*. Nor of the narrator of Daphne du Maurier's *Rebecca* who has such a hard time at Manderley as the second Mrs de Winter – Rebecca being the first.

4 THE ONLY NOVELS THEIR AUTHORS WROTE

Lockwood and Nelly Dean between them narrate *Wuthering Heights*, the only novel by Emily Brontë, who was thirty when she died in 1848.

*The Bell Jar*, Sylvia Plath's only novel, was published in Britain in 1963, a month before she died – also aged thirty. Because of its autobiographical candour, complete with frank descriptions of depression and mental hospitals, the book came out here under the pseudonym Victoria Lucas. It wasn't published at all in America until 1971, because her mother feared it would embarrass Plath's friends, several of whom appear in thinly-disguised form. (The family mightn't have been best pleased either.)

Scarlett O'Hara is the heroine of *Gone With The Wind*, the only novel by Margaret Mitchell. (Despite the claims of the publishers when it came out in 1996, a short story she'd written when she was sixteen doesn't count.) In 1949, thirteen years after its publication, Mitchell was knocked down and killed by a car in Atlanta. Even before the 1939 film the book was already a big bestseller. It went on to become one of the biggest of the century.

In 1953 Churchill won the Nobel Prize for Literature for his historical works. His only novel, *Savrola*, had been published in 1900 and was a political/adventure tale set in the fictional country of Laurania.

And if *To Kill a Mockingbird* hadn't already been used for another connections question, it could also have been in this one. Published in 1961, it became another of the twentieth century's biggest bestsellers – yet Lee (who's still alive as of 2008) hasn't written so much as a paragraph of fiction since.

# Round Five

## Body of Literature: a Biological Round

1 *White Teeth* by Zadie Smith

2 *Jaws* by Peter Benchley. After the colossal success of the book, Peter Benchley tried for a while to show there was more to him than sharks – partly by writing *The Beast*, which was about a giant squid. His later books, though, included *Shark Trouble*, *White Shark*, *Shark Life* and *Shark!*

3 'I sing of arms and the man'. (In Latin, the phrase is '*Arma virumque cano*', once translated by Billy Bunter as 'The armed man with the dog'.)

4 'Heads' – the two main characters are playing a coin-tossing game where the coin keeps coming down heads

5 *My Left Foot*

6 *The Lovely Bones*

7 *Bury My Heart at Wounded Knee*

8 Mavis Cheek

9 *Fingersmith*

10 *Prick Up Your Ears* (Given the subject matter, it's possible that two body parts are intended to be heard there – neither of them 'ears'.)

# Quiz Ten

## Round One

### Books and Buildings

1 Which literary building is owned by the Earls of Groan?

2 In A. A. Milne's book of that name, who lives in the house at Pooh Corner?

3 Who wrote the novel *The House of the Seven Gables*?

4 Who drew on her American-frontier childhood for the *Little House on the Prairie* series?

5 Whose first novel was *Behind the Scenes at the Museum*?

6 Whose fifth novel was *The Hotel New Hampshire*?

7 In which literary work would you find Doubting Castle?

8 Which American poet's second collection was *Lord Weary's Castle* – which includes one of his best-known poems, 'The Quaker Graveyard in Nantucket'?

9 Who wrote the novella *The Ballad of the Sad Café*?

10 In Roald Dahl's *James and the Giant Peach*, where does the peach finally come to rest?


Answers on p. 275

## Round Two

### Did *You* Get That Far? Last Lines (that Maybe Not Everybody Reaches)

Fittingly enough, the final extracts round features the final sentences of some very famous books. The twist is that they're also the sort of books that not all readers will necessarily have made it to the final sentences of. Using your skill, judgement and perhaps even knowledge, can you identify the book and author in each case . . .

1 A novel of the 1860s:

> Just as in astronomy the difficulty of admitting the motion of the earth lay in the immediate sensation of the earth's stationariness, so in history the difficulty of recognising the subjection of the personality to the laws of space and time and causation lies in the difficulty of surmounting the direct sensation of the independence of one's personality.
>
> In the first case, we had to surmount the sensation of an unreal immobility in space, and to admit a motion we could not perceive of by sense. In the present case, it is as essential to surmount a consciousness of an unreal freedom and to recognise a dependence not perceived by our senses.



2 A non-fiction book of 1988:

> If we do discover a complete theory, it should in time be understandable in broad principle by everyone, not just a few scientists. Then we shall all,



Answers on p. 277

philosophers, scientists, and just ordinary people, be able to take part in the discussion of the question of why it is that we and the universe exist. If we find the answer to that, it would be the ultimate triumph of human reason – for then we would know the mind of God.

3 A seventeenth-century novel:

I shall be proud and satisfied to have been the first author to enjoy the full effect of his own writing. For my sole object has been to arouse men's contempt for the all fabulous and absurd stories of knight errantry, whose credit this tale has already shaken, and which will, without a doubt, soon tumble to the ground. Farewell.

4 A work of history completed in 1787:

The historian may applaud the importance and variety of his subject; but, while he is conscious of his own imperfections, he must often accuse the deficiency of his materials. It was among the ruins of the Capitol, that I first conceived the idea of a work which has amused and exercised near twenty years of my life, and which, however inadequate to my own wishes, I finally deliver to the curiosity and candour of the Public.

5 A biography of 1791:

When there was an audience, his real opinions could seldom be gathered from his talk; though when he was in company with a single friend, he would dis-

Answers on pp. 277–8

cuss a subject with genuine fairness; but he was too conscientious to make an error permanent and pernicious, by deliberately writing it; and in all his numerous works, he earnestly inculcated what appeared to him to be the truth; his piety being constant, and the ruling principle of all his conduct.

Such was -- --, a man whose talents, acquirements, and virtues were so extraordinary, that the more his character is considered, the more he will be regarded by the present age, and by posterity, with admiration and reverence.

6 A novel of the early twentieth century (and the last word of this punishingly long closing sentence is probably the biggest clue):

But at least, if strength were granted me for long enough to accomplish my work, I should not fail, even if the results were to make them resemble monsters, to describe men first and foremost as occupying a place, a very considerable place compared with the restricted one which is allotted to them in space, a place on the contrary prolonged past measure – for simultaneously, like giants plunged into the years, they touch epochs that are immensely far apart, separated by the slow accretion of many, many days – in the dimension of Time.



 Answers on p. 278

# Round Three

## Featured Author: Charles Dickens

1 In *Oliver Twist*, as whom is John Dawkins better known?

2 Which of his novels did Dickens say was his own favourite?

3 Dickens's fourth novel was the first he'd published not to have the main character's name in the title. What was it?

4 In *A Christmas Carol*, who's Tiny Tim's father?

5 What are the first twelve words of *A Tale of Two Cities*?

6 (Quite a hard one admittedly) Which Dickens novel has a plot that centres on someone leaving money to his nephew's lover's guardian's brother's youngest daughter?

7 In which Dickens novel would you find the characters Mr Chadband, Mr Snagsby, Mrs Jellyby and Mr Turveydrop?

Q10

8 Complete this piece of Dickens criticism by Oscar Wilde: 'One must have a heart of stone to read the death of Little Nell . . .'

9 What novel did Dickens leave unfinished at the time of his death?



Answers on p. 279

10 When Dickens died was he fifty-eight, sixty-eight or seventy-eight?

Answers on p. 279

## Round Four

### A Round on the Links: Literary Connections

Can you link the following literary people or things?

1 (Maybe one for the dads)
*The Wasp Factory*
*The Lonely Passion of Judith Hearne*
Brother Cadfael
Twice over, the birthplace of Walter de la Mare

2 Henry Perowne, neurosurgeon
The late Jack Dodds, Bermondsey butcher
Leopold Bloom
Clarissa Dalloway

3 *Flowers in the Attic*
*A Streetcar Named Desire*
'Rip Van Winkle'
Louise Rennison's confessions of a teenage girl

Q10

4 Finally, and appropriately:
Giles Foden's first novel
Nikos Kazantzakis controversially fictionalises the life of Jesus


Answers on pp. 281–4

Uncas in a novel by James Fenimore Cooper

Scott Fitzgerald's unfinished novel about Hollywood

# Round Five

## And Finally: Literary Lasts, Conclusions and Farewells

1 Who wrote the autobiographical novel *Goodbye to Berlin*?

2 Who wrote the controversial novel *Last Exit to Brooklyn*?

3 Which historian made his name in 1947 with *The Last Days of Hitler*?

4 Who wrote the much-anthologised poem 'My Last Duchess'?

5 What's the last novel in Philip Pullman's *His Dark Materials* trilogy?

6 What's the last (and Booker-winning) novel in Pat Barker's *Regeneration* trilogy?

7 Who wrote the First World War play *Journey's End*?

8 Which poem ends:

> A sadder and a wiser man,
> He rose the morrow morn.

9 Whose autobiography was entitled *Goodbye to All That*?

10 What are the last four words spoken by Hamlet?

Q10

 Answers on p. 285

# Quiz Ten: Answers

## Round One

### Books and Buildings

1 Gormenghast, in the books by Mervyn Peake

2 Eeyore

3 Nathaniel Hawthorne

4 Laura Ingalls Wilder. *Little House on the Prairie* itself was the second in the series – and much debate still rages as to whether the books, written in the third person, are straight autobiography or autobiographical fiction.

5 Kate Atkinson

6 John Irving

7 *The Pilgrim's Progress* by John Bunyan

8 Robert Lowell

9 Carson McCullers – who rather specialised in striking titles. Her novels include *The Heart Is a Lonely Hunter* and *Reflections in a Golden Eye*. She also wrote a play called *The Square Root of Wonderful* and a collection of poems called *Sweet as a Pickle and Clean as a Pig*.

10 On top of the Empire State Building

## Round Two

### Did *You* Get That Far? Last Lines (that Maybe Not Everybody Reaches)

1 Leo Tolstoy pondering the nature of history, and free will versus determinism in the less-than-punchy final sentences of *War and Peace* – possibly the daddy of them all when it comes to not-always-read bestsellers. Still, you could always follow the example of Woody Allen who once explained that: 'I took a speed-reading course and read *War and Peace* in twenty minutes. It's about Russia.'

2 The rousing finale to Stephen Hawking's *A Brief History of Time*, which spent a record 237 weeks on the *Sunday Times* bestseller lists. One reason for its success may have been that Hawking reluctantly followed the advice he was given that 'each equation I included in the book would halve the sales'. In the end, he put in only one: $E=mc^2$.

3 The closing words of *Don Quixote* by Miguel de Cervantes. According to Martin Amis, 'While clearly an impregnable masterpiece, *Don Quixote* suffers from one fairly serious flaw – that of outright unreadability. The book bristles with beauties, charm, sublime comedy; it is also, for long stretches (approaching about 75 per cent of the whole), inhumanly dull.'

4 Edward Gibbon reaching the end of *The History of the Decline and Fall of the Roman Empire*. In that passage you can almost hear his sigh of relief – but he later wrote, rather poignantly, that his initial sense of freedom at finishing the book was followed by a feeling of melancholy at taking 'an everlasting leave of an old and agreeable companion'.

5 James Boswell paying a final tribute to his subject and friend in *The Life of Samuel Johnson*. Just in case you're wondering, Johnson's opinions couldn't be trusted when there was an audience, because 'from a spirit of contradiction, and a delight in showing his powers, he would often maintain the wrong side with equal warmth and ingenuity'.

6 The end of the final volume of Marcel Proust's *À la recherche du temps perdu* – which means that sentence comes on the three thousand two hundred and ninety-fourth page of the three-volume Penguin edition.

## Round Three

### Featured Author: Charles Dickens

1 The Artful Dodger

2 *David Copperfield*. The year before his death Dickens wrote a preface to the novel which contained this touching admission: 'Of all my books, I like this the best. I am a fond parent to every child of my fancy . . . But, like many fond parents, I have in my heart of hearts a favourite child. And his name is *David Copperfield*.'

3 *The Old Curiosity Shop* – the first three being *The Pickwick Papers*, *Oliver Twist* and *Nicholas Nickleby*

4 Bob Cratchit

5 'It was the best of times, it was the worst of times.'

6 *Little Dorrit*. (To be strictly ethical, it should be acknowledged that this description of the plot comes from *The Information* by Martin Amis.)

7 *Bleak House*

8 '. . . without laughing.'

9 *The Mystery of Edwin Drood*

10 Fifty-eight

# Round Four

## A Round on the Links: Literary Connections

1 NAMES OF THE MEMBERS OF ENGLAND'S 1966 WORLD CUP-WINNING SIDE

*The Wasp Factory* was the first novel by Iain Banks, as in Gordon.

*The Lonely Passion of Judith Hearne*, about an Irish spinster, is by Brian Moore, as in Bobby. The novel was originally called just *Judith Hearne* in Britain – but its American title has since caught on here too.

Brother Cadfael was the crime-solving mediaeval monk in the novels of Ellis Peters (as in Martin), one of the many pseudonyms used by Edith Pargeter, whose work ranged from Czech translations to war stories. Her first Cadfael novel was written when she was sixty-three, but around twenty more followed.

De la Mare was born in 1873 in Charlton (then in Kent, now part of South London) – which was needed twice over because both Bobby and Jack Charlton were in the team.



2 THE MAIN CHARACTERS OF NOVELS WHOSE ACTION LASTS FOR ONE DAY

Henry Perowne is the protagonist of *Saturday* – Ian McEwan's novel set on Saturday 15 February 2003, the day of the demonstrations in London against the Iraq war.

Jack Dodds is – sort of – the main character of *Last Orders* by Graham Swift, because his are the ashes being carried to Margate by his friends on the day the novel describes.

Leopold Bloom is in James Joyce's *Ulysses*, set in Dublin on 16 June 1904, the day Joyce had had his first date with his future lover and eventually wife, Nora Barnacle. (The book's publication date was personally significant too: 2 February 1922 was Joyce's fortieth birthday.)

Clarissa Dalloway is the heroine of Virginia Woolf's *Mrs Dalloway*, which follows her through a day on which she's hosting a party.

### 3 PEOPLE WITH THE SAME FIRST NAMES AS AMERICAN STATES

*Flowers in the Attic* is the 1979 bestseller by Virginia Andrews. She later became so successful that after she died in 1986 her estate hired a ghost writer to continue producing books in her name.

Tennessee Williams's *A Streetcar Named Desire* is the play featuring faded Southern belle Blanche DuBois having a rough time in New Orleans – until she's led off to a mental hospital with her farewell line: 'I have always depended on the kindness of strangers.'

'Rip Van Winkle' is a story by Washington Irving, about a man in New York's Catskill mountains who falls asleep for twenty years. When he wakes up, he discovers that the American Revolution has taken place. He also discovers that his nagging wife is dead – which makes some of the village's other hen-pecked husbands wish they'd been so lucky.

*Confessions of Georgia Nicolson* is Louise Rennison's series for teenage girls, and huge in both Britain and America, where her fans meet to 'talk British'. The series began with *Angus, Thongs and Full-Frontal Snogging*, and later titles include *It's OK, I'm Wearing Really Big Knickers*, *Dancing in My Nuddy Pants* and *Knocked Out by My Nunga-Nungas*.

4 LITERARY LASTS

(Appropriately, because it's the last connections question in the book)

Giles Foden's *The Last King of Scotland* (1998) was about Idi Amin, who claimed that title for himself when he was president of Uganda. In the film of the book, Foden had a cameo role as a journalist.

Kazantzakis's *The Last Temptation of Christ* (1951) depicted Jesus struggling with fears and doubts – and was soon placed on the Index of Prohibited Books by the Vatican. Martin Scorsese's film version of 1988 caused a similar fuss, especially among born-again Christians in America. (Kazantzakis's *Zorba the Greek* made for a less controversial film, and launched a thousand package tours instead.)

Uncas is the Last of the Mohicans in Cooper's 1826 novel of that name.

Fitzgerald's *The Last Tycoon* was left unfinished when he died suddenly in 1940. The book drew on his time as a Hollywood scriptwriter and the movie mogul of the title, Monroe Stahr, was closely modelled on Irving Thalberg.

# Round Five

## And Finally: Literary Lasts, Conclusions and Farewells

1 Christopher Isherwood. *Goodbye to Berlin* and Isherwood's earlier book *Mr Norris Changes Trains* were the basis of the musical *Cabaret*.

2 Hubert Selby Jr. In 1966, the book was successfully prosecuted in Britain under the Obscene Publications Act, when one of the witnesses for the prosecution was Robert Maxwell. The verdict was overturned two years later in an appeal brought by John Mortimer. (Chapter Two of *Last Exit to Brooklyn*, by the way, is called 'The Queen Is Dead' – which is where the Smiths got the title of their most highly acclaimed album.)

3 Hugh (or H. R.) Trevor-Roper – who did much to unmake his name thirty-six years later when he declared the forged Hitler diaries to be genuine.

4 Robert Browning

5 *The Amber Spyglass*

6 *The Ghost Road*

7 R. C. Sherriff

8 'The Rime of the Ancient Mariner' by Samuel Taylor Coleridge

9 Robert Graves

10 'The rest is silence.'

1 From 'Locksley Hall' by Alfred, Lord Tennyson

2 From *Heart of Darkness* by Joseph Conrad

3 From 'An Essay on Criticism' by Alexander Pope

4 From 'Meditation XVII' by John Donne

5 From 'If' by Rudyard Kipling

6 From 'Pippa Passes' by Robert Browning

# Acknowledgements

The rounds of literary mistakes draw partly on a section in *Flaubert's Parrot* by Julian Barnes, which in turn drew on (and led me to) a helpful lecture by Christopher Ricks.

My warmest thanks to all those involved in *The Write Stuff* over the years, including:

The endlessly impressive team captains, John Walsh and Sebastian Faulks – who, you might be depressed to hear, get almost all the questions right. (They don't have any prior knowledge of them either, even if the radio reviewer in the *Guardian* once suggested that they must do. Not that I'm bitter about that or anything.)

The producers – Jon Rolph, Dawn Ellis and Katie Marsden – for all their support, and for all the fun we've had.

The readers, Becky Hindley and Beth Chalmers.

All the guests.

All the people who've worked so hard behind the scenes (in the traditional way, too numerous to mention).

John Pidgeon, Paul Schlesinger, Caroline Raphael and Mark Damazer at Radio 4.

Finally, many thanks as ever to Helen, who did too much of the work looking after Sam while I was writing all this – and yet who still found time to make valuable suggestions.

# Permissions

(no peeking before doing the quizzes)

The author and publishers gratefully acknowledge permission granted to reproduce extracts from the following books in this volume:

*Arthur and George* by Julian Barnes, published by Jonathan Cape, 2005, © Julian Barnes, 2005. Reprinted by permission of The RandomHouse Group Ltd.

'Royal Wedding' by John Betjeman, © John Betjeman 1981. Reproduced by permission of Aitken Alexander Associates.

*The History Man* by Malcolm Bradbury (Secker & Warburg, 1975) © Malcolm Bradbury, 1975. Reprinted by permission of Pan Macmillan, London.

*Possession* by A. S. Byatt, published by Chatto & Windus, 1990, © A. S. Byatt, 1990. Reprinted by permission of The RandomHouse Group Ltd.

A letter by John le Carré published in the *Guardian* on 21 November 1997. Reproduced by permission of David Higham Associates.

*Diaries* by Alan Clark (Weidenfeld & Nicolson, a division of The Orion Publishing Group, 1993) © Alan Clark, 1993. Reproduced by permission of The Orion Publishing Group.

*William, Prime Minister* by Richmal Crompton, originally published in *William the Outlaw* (George Newnes, 1927), © Richmal Crompton, 1927. Reproduced by permission of AP Watt Ltd on behalf of Dr Paul Ashbee.

*Birdsong* by Sebastian Faulks, published by Hutchinson, 1993, © Sebastian Faulks, 1993. Reprinted by permission of The RandomHouse Group Ltd.

*Bridget Jones's Diary* by Helen Fielding (Picador, 1996) © Helen Fielding, 1996. Reprinted by permission of Pan Macmillan, London.

*Lord of the Flies* by William Golding (Faber and Faber Ltd, 1954) © William Golding, 1954. Reprinted by permission of Faber and Faber Ltd.

*The Smoking Diaries* by Simon Gray (Granta, 2004) © Simon Gray, 2004.

*Fatherland* by Robert Harris, published by Hutchinson, 1992, © Robert Harris, 1992. Reprinted by permission of RandomHouse Group Ltd.

*Red Dragon* by Thomas Harris, published by The Bodley Head, 1982, © Thomas Harris, 1981. Reprinted by permission of The RandomHouse Group Ltd.

*A Brief History of Time* by Stephen Hawking, published by Bantam Press, 1988, © Space Time Publications, 1988. Reprinted by permission of The RandomHouse Group Ltd.

A letter from Ernest Hemingway to Scott Fitzgerald, written on 1 July 1925, reprinted with the permission of Scribner, a Division of Simon & Schuster, Inc., from *Ernest Hemingway: Selected Letters, 1917–1961*, edited by Carlos Baker © Hemingway Foreign Rights Trust.

*About a Boy* by Nick Hornby (Victor Gollancz, 1998) © Nick Hornby, 1998. Reproduced by permission of Penguin Books Ltd.

*Lady Chatterley's Lover* by D. H. Lawrence (First full edition Penguin Books, 1960) © The Estate of D. H. Lawrence 1960. Reproduced by permission of Pollinger Limited and the Estate of Frieda Lawrence Ravagli.

*On Chesil Beach* by Ian McEwan, published by Jonathan Cape, 2007, © Ian McEwan, 2007. Reprinted by permission of The RandomHouse Group Ltd.

*Stupid White Men* by Michael Moore (Penguin Books, 2002) © Michael Moore 2001, 2002. Reproduced by permission of Penguin Books Ltd.

*Lolita* by Vladimir Nabokov (Weidenfield & Nicolson, 1959) © Vladimir Nabokov, 1955. Reproduced by permission of Penguin Books Ltd.

*The Remembrance of Things Past* by Marcel Proust, translated C K Scott Moncrieff and Terence Kilmartin, published by Chatto & Windus, 1954. Translation © Chatto & Windus and RandomHouse, Inc, 1981. Reprinted by permission of The RandomHouse Group Ltd.

Speech at Moscow's Trade Union Central Hall by George Bernard Shaw, published in *Bernard Shaw: the Definitive One-Volume Edition* by Michael Holroyd (Vintage, 1997) © Michael Holroyd, 1997. Reproduced by permission of The Society of Authors, on behalf of the Bernard Shaw Estate.

*The Hundred and One Dalmatians* by Dodie Smith. Text copyright © the Estate of Dodie Smith 1956. Published by Egmont UK Ltd London and used with permission.

*The Autograph Man* by Zadie Smith (Hamish Hamilton, 2002) © Zadie Smith, 2002. Reproduced by permission of Penguin Books Ltd.

*The Prime of Miss Jean Brodie* by Muriel Spark (Macmillan, 1961) © Muriel Spark 1961. Reproduced by permission of David Higham Associates Limited.

*Anna Karenina* by Leo Tolstoy, translated by Rosemary Edmonds (Penguin Books, 1954) Translation © Rosemary Edmonds, 1954. Reproduced by permission of Penguin Books Ltd.

*War and Peace* by Leo Tolstoy, translated by Constance Garnett (Heinemann, 1904), translation © Constance Garnett, 1904. Reproduced by permission of AP Watt Ltd on behalf of the Executors of the Estate of Constance Garnett.

*Adrian Mole: The Cappuccino Years* by Sue Townsend (Michael Joseph, 1999) © Sue Townsend, 1999. Reproduced by permission of Penguin Books Ltd.

'Rodney Has a Relapse' from the collection *Nothing Serious* by P. G. Wodehouse (Herbert Jenkins, 1950) © The Trustees of the Wodehouse Estate Rogers, 1950. Reproduced by permission of Rogers, Coleridge & White Ltd.

*The Bonfire of the Vanities* by Tom Wolfe (1987), published by Jonathan Cape, 1987, © Tom Wolfe, 1987.

Reprinted by permission of The RandomHouse Group Ltd.

*The Diary of Virginia Woolf*, vol 2, by Virginia Woolf published by Hogarth Press. Used by permission of the executors of the Virginia Woolf Estate and The RandomHouse Group Limited.

All reasonable efforts have been made by the author and the publisher to trace the copyright holders of the material quoted in the book. In the event that the author or publisher are contacted by any of the untraceable copyright holders after the publication of this book, the author and publisher will endeavour to rectify the position accordingly.